Cameron,
thank you for
your time.
Much love,
Maria
12/20/20

a COURSE in LEADERSHIP

21 spiritual lessons on power, love and influence

DR. MARIA CHURCH

AUTHOR OF *LOVE-BASED LEADERSHIP*

DUDLEY COURT PRESS
SONOITA, AZ

Published in the United States of America by
Dudley Court Press
PO Box 102 Sonoita, AZ 85637
www.DudleyCourtPress.com

Cover and interior design by Dunn+Associates, www.Dunn-Design.com

Publisher's Cataloging-in-Publication Data
Names: Church, Maria, 1961- author.

Title: A course in leadership : 21 spiritual lessons on power, love, and influence / Dr. Maria Church.

Description: Sonoita, Arizona : Dudley Court Press, [2021]
Identifiers: ISBN: 978-1-940013-70-1
978-1-940013-71-8 (ebook)
978-1-940013-72-5 (audio)
LCCN: 2020925953

Subjects:
LCSH: Leadership. | Spirituality. | Authentic leadership. | Awareness.
Intuition. | Interpersonal relations. | Interpersonal communication. | Influence (Psychology)
Success. | Success in business. | Self-actualization (Psychology) |
BISAC: BUSINESS & ECONOMICS / Leadership.
BUSINESS & ECONOMICS / Business Ethics.
SELF-HELP / Personal Growth / Success.
Classification: LCC: HD57.7 .C48 2020
DDC: 658.4/092—dc23

To connect with Maria Church, please visit www.DrMariaChurch.com

Look for other books in this series at your favorite bookseller
or at www.DudleyCourtPress.com

For Melissa.
You are the beautiful embodiment
of a grace-filled, love-based leader.

Contents

Foreword

As I write this, the world has just watched in real time one of the most frightening leadership breakdowns of its longest-standing democracy. If there was any lingering doubt, or we all simply needed reminding what fear-based leadership can bring about, let the newspaper covers across the world showing rioters breaching the U.S. Capitol building be the wake-up call.

It is impossible to ignore the divine timing of this book, as well as the rich irony that you're not supposed to talk in business about the things Dr. Maria Church discusses in this book. You're not supposed to talk about love or spiritual teachings or atonement, let alone God. And you're most certainly not to bring these topics into leadership development or, gasp, into business growth strategy.

Yet, tearing down that barrier is exactly what Dr. Church boldly accomplishes in this book.

At its core, this book is about providing the blueprint for leaders to attain the ultimate reconnection—both for themselves as well as for those they lead. So it's fitting then that this book also comes on the heels of a year when the world rediscovered the essential bond of human-to-human connection, all because we were forced to be physically apart.

Admittedly, when I first met Dr. Church a number of years ago and she began to share her perspectives on leadership, I was a bit skeptical. Not because what she was saying wasn't true. On the contrary, she writes nothing but truth. I was a skeptic because I didn't know if leaders were ready to hear it, much less embrace it. I'm humbled to admit that not only was I wrong, but furthermore, that leaders are indeed *yearning* for this level of truth.

For the last six years, I've watched as Dr. Church has guided executives and organizations to reexamine core beliefs about what it means to lead. I've seen firsthand the results, the data, and the anecdotes of her work in action, and it is nothing short of groundbreaking.

With that knowledge, there are three reasons I believe this book will turn the tide in the way leaders lead both themselves and others. First, Dr. Church's book is written in the total absence of fear. To be clear, when writing about spirituality, particularly in the context of business, many fear issues could potentially arise. But Dr. Church makes no such calculations or apologies in her writing. This book is the definition of a courageous conversation.

Second, her book is accessible, practical, and actionable. After more than three decades in the professional world, working on the front lines of leadership in government, nonprofit, higher education, corporate America, and entrepreneurship, Dr. Church has had thousands of conversations with real leaders like you, and has faced very real challenges that don't fit neatly into a textbook and that cannot be solved with leadership clichés.

The pages of this book are filled with highly relatable examples. The exercises, activities, and tools are not literary devices but rather real-world techniques Dr. Church utilizes with her firm's clients—courageous executives and leaders boldly achieving lasting transformations in their organizations—to affect real change.

Third, and most importantly, this book provides a new—and much needed—North Star. Since the 1930s when social scientists first began to examine the concept of leadership and the idea that it's something that can be taught, progress has been incremental at best. Yet, as is evidenced by the news each and every day, the world is in desperate need of a leadership *revolution*.

To that end, and as Dr. Church points out in this book, we can no longer try to compartmentalize our lives. There's no such thing as a personal life versus a work life, any more than we can fragment our beings into our intellectual selves versus our spiritual selves.

In order to move the business world beyond the same challenges that have plagued it for more than 100 years, leaders must finally embrace and lead from the ultimate truth: we are all spiritual beings on parallel quests. This book serves as the map to shifting fully into that new and uncorroded perspective.

One final word: Many people, no doubt you included, will read this book, learn its spiritual lessons, and come to love the results of those lessons on your leadership journey. I am blessed, however, to have the added privilege of getting to know and coming to love the book's author as well.

A couple of years ago, I had the blessed fortune to spend a few days on Necker Island, along with its owner, Sir Richard Branson, several world leaders, and about two dozen fellow change agents, including Dr. Church. During that life-altering experience, I got to know Maria on a level one doesn't typically ever get to know a client or, for that matter, even a friend.

Over the course of those spiritually awakening, highly conscious days and nights, what I discovered in Maria was a rare soul, pure in her fidelity of mission and purpose. Both a leader and a follower. A soulful being who is the complete and total embodiment of her message. So, with that knowledge I can say to you that every word on these pages is written humbly, in service to both you and the world, and imbued with love.

—Angelique Rewers
CEO, The Corporate Agent

INTRODUCTION

The leader and the follower emerge as separate roles, each seeming to possess advantages you would not want to lose. So in their fusion there appears to be the hope of satisfaction and of peace . . . Be very still an instant. Come without all thought of what you ever learned before, and put aside all images you made. The old will fall away before the new, without your opposition or intent.

~ A Course in Miracles

This course in leadership is for leaders who are looking for a way to integrate spirituality with leadership. This text is not a religious doctrine, although I present spiritual insight and wisdom from many thinkers. This text is not a theoretical discourse, although I include concepts from different academic models. This is a course on *leadership*, and at various stages of our lives, all of us are leaders, followers, or both.

This course honors those who went before us—the ancestors, those distant teachers whose wisdom is cited in this text, and those leaders and teachers who currently lead in life. The blessings they share with us appear throughout this course. Honored, too, are those who carry the knowledge, wisdom, and lessons forward in legacy as beacons of love-based leadership.

A Course in Leadership is based in part on fundamental principles of love, fear, ego, God, and miracles. Believing that we are both leaders and followers conceptually, we are simultaneously both leaders and followers of our own life. We lead our lives by the choices we make to follow the paths of either love *or* fear.

This same juxtaposition of both leading and following is prevalent in our family and work lives. *A Course in Leadership* integrates all aspects of our lives, removes the taught models of compartmentalization, and approaches our leadership and followership in wholeness, including our spirituality. This course and text is not about the latest buzzwords, tools, or techniques we may apply at work. Instead, through understanding the spiritual connection that leadership and love have in our day-to-day activities, we experience right-mindedness and readiness to embrace miracles in all aspects of leadership, love, and life.

Let's take a moment and frame a few basic concepts and terminology interwoven throughout this text:

1. *Love is God.*

   I have chosen to use the term *God* in this text, which in no way implies any religious or denominational identity. As I speak of God, I speak of Source, Universe, Great Spirit, Higher Power, Higher Self, or any other representation you may affix to the collective power of love and unity, greater than our individual selves. As I speak on love, I am talking about the universal concept of love, not a romantic state. This is the love we have for one another in collective unity with honor, care, trust, and compassion.

2. *Love is the antithesis of fear.*

   Fear and love cannot exist simultaneously. Where fear exists, love is not present, and when love exists, fear cannot emerge. Fear and love are not sister or companion states, and they can never coexist. Perfect love drives out all fear . . . and love is perfect.

3. *Fear is ego.*

   Different from our psychology class definition that indicates a need for the ego, the sole purpose of our egos is to separate us from our natural state of love. Just as love and fear cannot exist together, ego and unity cannot coexist either. Where love joins, ego divides.

4. *Miracles are shifts in perceptions from fear to love.*

   This definition of miracles is so simply stated and yet profound in its magnitude. As we explore miracles throughout this text, we see miracles and miracle workers emerging in our lives every day.

5. *We are all both leaders and followers.*

At different times throughout our lives, we find that we are leaders, followers, or sometimes both. At the most basic, fundamental level, we are all leaders of our own lives.

We must view leading with ethics and values beyond a strictly theoretical and religious domain. Existing leadership and business models representing the ways we conduct business and lead organizations are no longer working; systems and structures are breaking down. We cannot turn on the news today without hearing how yet another leader has harmed people, organizations, or even nations. Ethics and behavior in leadership positions are legislated, and prominent figures are going to jail for irresponsible leadership. We must stop the insanity! Einstein warned us that insanity is trying to solve problems with the same strategies that created the problems in the first place. We must lead in a different way with our lives, our families, our communities, and our countries.

In over three decades in the workforce, I've experienced leadership firsthand in corporate America, government, non-profits, and academia. Having taught leadership courses for over a decade, I know we are hungry for a better way to lead our organizations and our lives. Clients with whom I work are looking for authentic and genuine ways to lead. We are all tired of checking our soul at the door of our organizations. We are exhausted from living and working in fear. Fear is sometimes easy to identify when it starts to creep in and our body becomes tense, blood pressure starts to rise, and feelings of anxiety emerge. Fear is not a good feeling, so why would we continue to go there?

Where love and spirit are *internal* to us, fear and ego are *external*. Turning to others for approval or acceptance points us in the direction of ego, external to ourselves. When we live in the past, we live in the ego. Reliving certain events involving our relationships with others can cause tremendous pain or hurt. Each time we choose—yes, it is a choice—to live in the space of fear, we give away our power. We give it away to people or circumstances—an external event. When we retain our power, we are empowered, and we then live in a place of love and spirit.

Fear paralyzes us. True, fear can be a motivator, but it is neither sustainable nor healthy.

We cannot be motivated and live in fear for long periods without paying the physical, emotional, and spiritual costs of fear and stress. In my book *Love-Based Leadership: The Model for Leading with Strength, Grace, and Authenticity*, I include a piece I wrote in the height of my leadership insanity:

> *I've done it! I accomplished whatever Mom and Dad told me I could do! I have arrived.*
>
> *As the firstborn of a pre–baby boomer couple, my parents always told me to do what makes me happy, and remember that I could accomplish anything. They supported my desire to pursue acting. They supported my desire to study sign language interpretation (I liked the dramatic flair), then they encouraged my business drive. My mother always had a career. She broke through many glass ceilings and earned great respect in her profession. She was my inspiration to break on through to the other side. I have arrived.*
>
> *When I moved up in my organization and took on more responsibility, I tripled my income over a nine-month period. In addition to the money, I earned respect and a place at the table with the men. Four men, and little ol' me. I had a place at the table in a predominately all-male industry. I have arrived.*

I changed my wardrobe, hair, and personal style. After all, I was in senior management. I have arrived.

I worked eighty hours a week. I was dealing in hundreds of thousands of dollars daily. I was getting little sleep with the worry. Yet, I felt important and needed; the men in my organization had come to depend on me and on my opinions. I have arrived.

I started to show symptoms of extreme stress. On my fortieth birthday, the doctor put me on blood pressure medicine and told me I needed to exercise more. I'd been working long hours and my eating habits were atrocious. Fast food eaten even faster became the norm. I took up smoking as a stress reliever (yes, I am an educated woman, and yes, I know the hazards of smoking). I have arrived.

One day, on my back patio after a long day at work, with a martini in one hand and a cigarette in the other, I had a thought, I have a place at the table. I have earned respect for my hard work and knowledge. I have an awesome six-figure income. I have everything the successful men have had for decades. I have 30 pounds of extra weight. I have a high-level position. I have a stressful job. I have a beautiful home. I have high blood pressure. I have a drink in one hand and a cigarette in the other. Oh my God—I do have it all! I have arrived ...

But just exactly where am I?[1]

This question, along with similar ponderings from my colleagues, clients, and students propelled me on a journey of discovery. For me, I found the answer in reconnecting with God; and the gift I received in my insight, a *miracle*.

I recently spoke at a women's business conference, a daylong seminar filled with presenters on various elements of compiling a business plan. Presenting an "add on" to the plan, I spoke about self-care as the most important asset in their businesses. After the presentation, a number of women came up to me expressing gratitude for including mind, body, and spirit into the presentation. One woman even said, "That was more inspiring and motivating than 10 AA meetings!" The positive reaction my presentation received reaffirmed to me that we are hungry and ready for a new way to lead our businesses and our lives.

> Surrender is to relax into the love in your heart as you face circumstances throughout your day.

Leadership is a tremendous responsibility, whether we lead organizations or lead our own lives. We co-create the lives we lead with God through surrender. Surrender is to relax into the love in your heart as you face circumstances throughout your day. While we have free will, it does not mean *we can establish the curriculum.* It does mean we choose when and how we live out our purpose and our divine will. We are free to choose—24/7 each day, every day.

While teaching leadership or marketing courses, I often have this thought: *Leading people and marketing are really the same activity. Isn't the primary objective of both to influence people in the direction of a goal?* True, marketing and leadership could sometimes be activities of manipulation and not of influence. We see and experience this manipulation in both marketing and leadership. Both *influence* and *manipulation* have power. The key is that only one has sustainability and comes from love. Manipulation comes from ego and can be an effective influencing tactic, but it is not sustaining; in fact, it is exhausting.

Influence, on the other hand, is nurturing, motivating, and full of momentum. To lead with influence requires the following:

- Authenticity – live in integrity, honesty, and truth
- Respect – we must give it to receive it
- Power – referent power, the power of respect, is sustaining
- Connection – most especially, active engagement through power listening
- Presence – showing up in mind, body, and spirit
- Honor and value – again, we must give it to receive it
- Strong sense of self – with a strong internal compass and vision
- Confidence – sometimes comes from experience, not to be confused with arrogance
- Wisdom – insight gained through self-reflection, not to be confused with education
- Love – feeling it, living it, and demonstrating it

In this text, bridging the leadership discussion with a spirituality discourse prepares leaders to live and lead to their highest potential, their highest self. Many leadership books present concepts such as strategic planning, thought leadership, goal setting, vision creating, and motivating others. Those concepts, juxtaposed with spirituality, are covered in this course as *awareness*, *intuition*, *order*, *intention*, and *relationships*.

Miracles await us as we discard the models of insanity and come into our right minds through *perception shifting*. We transform talking to *power listening*, routine to *openness*, mindlessness to *mindfulness*, obsession to *passion*, entitlement to *gratitude*, obscenity to *grace*, weightiness to *laughter*, routine to *creativity*, dis-ease to *health*, reduction to *growth*, knowledge to *wisdom*, telling to *teaching*, manipulation to *service*, division to *forgiveness*, and fear to *love*.

Book Map

Each of the *21 Lessons on Leadership* begins with the lesson content, Teachings, Thoughts, and Theories. Following the lesson is a section for Practice. This is where I share activities, exercises, and tools that you may use to develop your leadership competencies. I use many of these exercises with clients and students in their own leadership development. You may want to use a journal or download the Action Guide for *A Course in Leadership* at *www.ACourseInLeadership.com* to do the practice work. I also include bonus activities, exercises, and tools in the Action Guide, so please make sure to download the guide.

Following each Practice section is our opportunity to Pause in a holy space and consciously connect with our Source, the Universe, with God. You may choose to meditate, pray, or journal at each pause, as this is your opportunity to connect with the lessons on a spiritual level.

As an executive leadership coach and a teacher, I like to begin courses with an assessment. Let's take a few moments and conduct a review of your current leadership thoughts, beliefs, and feelings.

Pull out your journal or the downloaded Action Guide to reflect on and answer the following questions:

▶ Describe what your ideal leader looks like, including characteristics, behaviors, and values.

▶ Describe how you currently lead in your life and in your organization.

- ▶ How would you like to lead? Be very specific with skills, characteristics, behaviors, attitudes, values, and vision.
- ▶ Identify any barriers to leading in this manner.
- ▶ If you could remove one obstacle or barrier today, what would it be? Why?
- ▶ What does your ideal organization look like, including mission, vision, and values?
- ▶ If you had unlimited resources, what would you do? Why?
- ▶ What feelings arise when you read these questions?

Mahatma Gandhi had a tremendous influence on Rev. Dr. Martin Luther King Jr., specifically in the nonviolent way he chose to live his life. King stated, "I became deeply fascinated by his campaigns of nonviolent resistance. As I delved deeper into the philosophy of Gandhi, my skepticism concerning the power of love gradually diminished, and I came to see for the first time its potency in the area of social reform."[2] Love is transformational, and it can transform our work, our lives, and our communities.

The holy instant is now. It is time.

Let us begin the journey.

Pause

You are now invited to pray, reflect, or meditate on . . .

Dear God,

Shine your glorious light on the path of our journey, and

burn brightly in our hearts.

Help us to be open

to experience miracles in

our leadership and in our lives.

Thank you for your love

and your light.

When fear creeps in,

boldly and gently

remind us of your love.

There is nothing to fear.

Only love is real.

Nothing else exists.

Amen.

1
LESSON
AWARENESS

Every human has four endowments—
self-awareness, conscience, independent will,
and creative imagination. These give us the
ultimate human freedom . . .
The power to choose, to respond, to change.

—Stephen R. Covey

The world is not a problem; the problem is our
unawareness.

—Bunty Bhagwan Shree Rajneesh

Teachings, Thoughts, and Theories

Have you ever driven away from home, only to look back to see if you remembered to shut the garage door? Or, perhaps you missed your turn because you were on autopilot? These are moments of unconsciousness. Frankly, the thought: *How did I drive here and not notice that turn*? is a scary one. Each time I have been in an accident when it was my fault, it was because I was not paying attention. I was not aware. Many of us live our lives on autopilot. We live our lives as human doings, and not as human *beings*.

How does this mindlessness translate to our leadership abilities? Not very well. To lead others to their fullest potential requires that first, we must learn to lead ourselves. Leadership growth, as with personal and spiritual growth, begins with a deep dive into awareness. All the executive coaching I do begins with self-awareness. Awareness, like breathing, is essential to life, to living, and to leading.

> Awareness, like breathing, is essential to life, to living, and to leading.

Without awareness, we are simply sleepwalking, unconsciously going through the motions of an unlived life. We live lives of joyless striving. Without awareness, we lack understanding, rendering us blind and unable to see with clarity. Sometimes, waking up is just too difficult with the incessant noise, chatter, and clutter in our lives. I've had clients say that practicing awareness is hard; however, living a joyless, unconscious life is even harder, or dare I say, it is *living hell*.

The funny thing is, with awareness and awakening, the chatter is illuminated, and we see the noise for what it really is—*noise*, nothing more, nothing less. With awareness, we can dismiss it, because we know and see what *it* is.

Awareness is foundational to leadership, love, and life. Awareness is the breath of life and the light in the darkness. Think of walking around a dark room, bumping into objects, and hurting yourself. You try to feel your way around the room, but you keep running into furniture. You find a light switch and turn it on. *Aha*—that *thing* you ran into, bruising your calf, is a coffee table. Turning on the light switch in the darkness is like turning on awareness in your life. Yes, you could choose to leave the switch off, but why would you want to?

Awareness is the breath of life and the light in the darkness.

Many benefits await us as we move into this powerful state of being. "When you contain control of the internal direction of your attention, you will no longer stand in shallow water but will launch out into the deep of life," written by Neville in the *Power of Awareness.*[3]

I worked with a client who wanted to improve her leadership skills. She was bright, an MBA, and in a mid- to high-level leadership position in her organization. She was proficient and knowledgeable about her job. She did, however, have challenges connecting with people in warm and friendly ways. We started working, as I always do, with awareness. While the spirit was willing, the growth of awareness was a daily practice of doing the work to bring her mind and body into alignment. We worked on her self-awareness with various exercises such as deep breathing, journaling, and mindfulness practice.

As she developed this skill of being aware, a whole new world opened up for her. She was so joy-filled in her practice of awareness, equating this recognition to opening a beautiful gift, only to find another gorgeous gift waiting for her. She asked me why more people didn't know about living in a state of awareness. Good question. The answer is *ego*.

An adversary to awareness, ego seeks to maintain unconsciousness, reinforcing separation from God and ultimately from one another. Moving into awareness requires an awareness mindset, recognizing and consciously making the decision to wake up from an unconscious state of being. This will take some practice if you've been in an unconscious state for a while. Exercising your awareness is like exercising your muscles. If you haven't exercised in a while, it takes some time and thoughtful practice to make movement part of your routine, your regular state of being.

Two types of awareness serve leaders well: inward self-awareness, and an outward awareness of others. Self-awareness, with further examination, is comprised of three different levels: mind, body, and spirit. Different spaces, yet they are so closely intertwined that they appear as one. As we start to examine the depths of ourselves, the ego is ready, willing, and sometimes able to reinforce the insanity-infused mantra of separateness. However, when we recognize this ego chatter, we can then name it and release it to God.

As we begin discovery of self-awareness, we unearth our true self and tap into inner truth. Sometimes, this descent into the depths of our inner being may feel uncomfortable. *"Aha!"* I say to myself when this happens to someone I am coaching, because I love these moments and encourage my clients to keep diving. Those *seat-stirring moments* are clues that we are about to experience growth, understanding, and clarity. The deeper we go, the closer we get to truth. Sometimes we must go through some murky water before we get to the treasure, but remember that you are not alone, and something amazing is waiting for you: the real you, the authentic you, the beautiful you.

The need to judge thoughts, feelings, and emotions has become part of our human experience, our ego experience. Again, the ego thrives on separation, thus separation into "good" or "bad" is almost second nature for many of us. As we reconnect with God and dispel the notion that we are separate from Him, we will grow into the practice of nonjudgment. Our thoughts, feelings, and other inner signals are neither good nor bad; they just *are*. When we give them meaning of good or bad, we are reinforcing the belief system of separateness, the belief system of ego. I've always loved the description of the acronym for EGO, Edging God Out. When we allow ego to be in charge, we are telling God we know He can't handle it on His own, and thus we do not allow space for Him.

Just as we apply nonjudgment to our thoughts and feelings, the same love applied to our body moves us closer to atonement with God. *At-one-ment* with God reinforces the fact that we are not simply our bodies. We occupy our bodies in our human experience, and as with any fabulous present, we want to care for the precious gift that is our body. Reconnecting with God reconnects our mind with our body and spirit, all wrapped in love. Now *that* is a gift to cherish.

Our spiritual quest to reconnect with God is due to our separation from Him. We learned to compartmentalize and segregate our lives into special life units or special relationships. We have our spiritual life, our play life, our personal life, and of course, our work life. Again, when we fragment and separate, we cannot possibly live a whole life, a true life, and a life connected to God. Our self-awareness will see this insanity and put us in a right mindset, allowing us to gain a deeper understanding of our spiritual selves in this human experience. When we develop understanding, we grow in meaning, because understanding is a conduit to derive meaningful experiences.

With self-awareness, we clarify our values and our vision with new purpose and direction. We no longer sleepwalk through life. As leaders, our responsibility is to lead movement with vision and conviction, or we are ineffective leaders. The beautiful aspect of this clarity is the meaningful way that we lead, inspire, and motivate others. It is through a meaning-filled life that we resonate with others, consciously connecting us with one another.

> It is through a meaning-filled life that we resonate with others, consciously connecting us with one another.

A miracle occurs when we increase our self-awareness: we also grow in awareness of others. When we love, honor, and respect ourselves, the natural progression is to do so with others, which moves us into our natural state of love. William Stafford, a great American poet, once said that a writer's job is to dig so deep into his own story that he reaches *everyone's* story. This harmony with others is a catalyst toward atonement with God. Awareness of others manifested through the channels of empathy, care, compassion, and of course love strengthens our ability to lead with authenticity.

The harmony with others is a natural state of love and, therefore, atonement with God. As described in my book *Love-Based Leadership: The Model for Leading with Strength, Grace, and Authenticity*, the innate progression of the love of self, aligned with love of Source, flows easily into love of others. When aligned with God, we align with the truth and are without separation. We therefore align with others, with no beginning and with no end. We are at one. We are at atonement.

Practice
Daily

How do we practice the art of awareness? The first step is to develop an *awareness mindset*. Think of awareness as you would think of breathing. Breath is required for life, just as awareness is required for meaningful living. Without awareness, we simply go through the motions. We are not truly living when we are not breathing in awareness.

A good start is to begin with practicing self-awareness, going *inward* instead of observing outward. Become conscious of your thoughts. Try not to judge them as good or bad; just become aware of them, and see them for what they are: *thoughts*. Learn to recognize when the ego tries to inject separation into your thoughts. Don't shove the unpleasant thoughts down, as this can do you more harm than good. Acknowledge them and release them into the loving hands of God. Surrender is not the end; it is the beginning.

One of the most effective steps in awareness is to just *stop*—stop thinking, doing, and planning. Just be still. You can start with just a few moments each day and build your time as you are ready. I remember July 5, 2010, as though it were yesterday. I believe it was one of those unusual times in my adult life (up to that point) where I completely stopped. It was a rare summer day in Arizona with a pleasant temperature in the high eighties. The sky was turquoise blue, and a few exceptionally white clouds dotted the sky. Beautiful rugged brown mountains sprinkled with green from the recent rains created a canvas that literally caught my breath. As the clouds moved across the sky, their shapes shifted in different patterns to my delight. Then, an exquisite monarch butterfly appeared and began to dance for me, dipping into the pool for cool summer refreshment. It was a moment that froze in time for me—a moment where I came into awareness of my being one with God.

Deeper

Develop awareness for warning signs from your body such as fatigue, stress, and strain. We have an incredible early-alert system wired in our bodies. However, when we are not aware and succumb to the noise and clutter that numbs us into unconscious sleepwalking, we miss the signals. We miss the signals until our bodies must break through the noise. When the body breaks through, we know it because it knocks us off our feet. One of my favorite body lessons came from Iyanla Vanzant, who recommends putting our bodies to sleep the same day we get them up. She also reminds us to put better food into our bodies than we put fuel into our cars. Good advice, indeed.[4]

Observation to Connect with Others

You may practice another great exercise for developing awareness at your next meeting. At the meeting, try to listen for what is *not* being said. Observe the way your team members talk and move, and especially watch and listen to them when they are not speaking. What comes to light that you may have previously missed? My clients experience profound *aha* moments when they practice this exercise and are amazed at how much previously they failed to notice. One client in particular, Clare, took action and participated in this exercise of observing others at one of her team meetings, notating her observations with a focus on what was not being said. At our next session, while recapping the results of this exercise, she said, "Wow, I can't believe how clueless and insensitive I was as I observed my team. I saw Jim's uncertainty and Mary's fear. I had to wonder how many times I stepped right over them before." We must, however, move into awareness without beating ourselves up. The good news is that once Clare moved out of self-judgment, she was so tuned into what her team was feeling that she was able to form deeper relationships with her colleagues and to be a more effective and impactful leader.

Pause

You are now invited to pray, reflect, or meditate on . . .

Dear God,

I thank you

for the gift of awareness,

the gift of self-awareness,

and the gift of my awareness of others.

I pray that I may discover

the blocks and barriers

to my own awareness

and release those to you.

I thank you for the at-one-ment with you and through you.

Amen.

2
LESSON
MINDFULNESS

Do not dwell in the past, do not dream of the future, concentrate the mind on the present moment.

—Buddha

Teachings, Thoughts, and Theories

Similar to awareness, mindfulness requires a deliberate process of slowing down. In the height of my corporate career, if someone had suggested to me that I slow down to speed up, I would have laughed myself off the chair and then asked them what they smoked for lunch! Only after a year of extreme growth and intense mindfulness practice did I fully understand the concept of slowing down to speed up.

When I speak of *speeding up*, I am not talking about going at a frenetic pace to try to get more tasks done. "Been there, done that!" *And* I have the hospital bill to prove it. I had already tried that impractical self-imposed expectation of working at an unrealistic pace and had paid the physical and emotional price. What I am talking about is greater capacity to accomplish more high-quality results with less effort. Does this sound too good to be true or too complicated a formula to learn? It is quite simple—all it requires is mindfulness.

Both the terms *mindfulness* and *awareness*, often used inter-changeably, have a subtle yet powerful distinction in leadership development. Awareness,

> Conscious awareness of what fills our mind, helps to control our manifested reality.

as learned in the previous lesson, is an awakening to what is happening internally and externally. Awareness requires action. Granted, that action oftentimes is the active intention to slow down. Mindfulness is a state of being.

We can first begin to understand the lesson of mindfulness by simply dissecting the word into its two components, *mind-full.* What fills our mind? The attention or awareness of what fills our mind is a powerful realization. Of course, to come into this realization, you must wrap awareness action around the process. Conscious awareness of what fills our mind, helps to control our manifested reality.

I am not just reiterating the power of attraction here, which is like the little engine that could (*I think I can, I think I can*). I am talking about the power of the mind, coupled with the resulting behavior that follows. Both our thoughts and behaviors change the energy that surrounds us, directly impacting those within our energetic field.

Think about the self-fulfilling prophecy or *Pygmalion Effect*, a common leadership theory about expectations and perception distortions taught in many MBA classes. This theory may have both positive and negative outcomes, depending on the expectation placed on an individual or group. As leaders, we consciously and unconsciously create expectations of those we lead. For example, suppose you believe that a member of your team is not able to fulfill a task, even before he begins, but you give him the task anyway. When you review the work he has done so far, you find it plagued with error and fault. As a result, he is a complete failure at the task, losing all confidence, hope, and self-efficacy for success. Mission accomplished—you were correct; he failed and was not able to fulfill the task.

Conversely, say you believe a team member will be highly successful on a new project she has never done before. You review the partial work submitted, you mentor, and you encourage her to keep up the great work. You help her and support her along the way. The outcome? You guessed it; she was successful in the work. What fills our mind is powerful and telling. We must be consciously aware of our expectations of ourselves and others so we do not succumb adversely to the Pygmalion Effect.

The leadership power of mindfulness is a heightened sense of awareness. The heightened state creates a sharp focus on our thoughts and on what fills our mind. With this focus, clutter naturally moves out of the way and provides clarity. Clarity is so fantastic when we achieve it, simplifying what was formerly complicated and muddled thinking. Clarity helps leaders in so many ways, from planning to communication and from understanding to vision. Clarity is awareness on steroids—in other words, clarity is mindfulness.

Planning with clarity allows leaders to see what needs to be done with simplicity, thus un-complicating a circumstance or situation. This phenomenon is almost as though, through mindful clarity, one becomes enlightened (unburdened, uncluttered) in their thoughts. A leader's *in-light-end* state gives the necessary clarity to plan and avert potential crises that arise when we experience lack of clarity, lack of planning, and procrastination in an overwhelmed state of mind.

Leaders can communicate and connect with others more efficiently and effectively when mindfulness is part of their consciousness. In other words, leaders who are mindful *show up*. I recently had a discussion with a client about how leaders "show up." He wasn't quite sure how to do it or describe it, but he clearly knew what it meant when someone showed up. We started to peel back the layers of what it meant to show up. He recognized that showing up meant to be attentive with good listening skills when someone was talking. As we dug deeper, he realized that showing up went beyond the well-learned, crafted way we demonstrate "good communication skills"— such as leaning forward, nodding our heads, and having great eye contact. Showing up meant being fully present in mind, body, and spirit; not just going through the motions of attentiveness, but being wholeheartedly present. With this realization, he started practicing *showing up*, and he quickly found that his connections with people at work (and home) became deeper and more substantive.

Mindful presence, or showing up, is being fully present when communicating. Full presence is conscious contact with God, yourself, and others and not rehashing in your mind the argument you had with your spouse before work or the phone call you need to make. Presence requires full attention and focus on what inhabits your mind.

Great leaders, who communicate and connect effectively, fill their minds with the person in front of them. We feel this connection when others are fully engaged in what we are saying. We see it in their eyes, we feel it energetically, we *know* we are connected and drawn to that person and the moment. Presence is mindfulness. Mindfulness is found in the present.

When we find this connection with others through mindfulness, we gain a deeper understanding of each other and ourselves. Of course we do, since we are *mind-full* of their presence in the moment. We also understand ourselves better when we connect with others. It is not unusual, with this deep union of souls, to see ourselves in those people with whom we feel connected. In a mindful state, empathy, connection, compassion, and equality surface to our consciousness. We see and feel each other as the same, without division and without judgment—we feel love.

When we love someone or something, we give it great value and care. One of the top reasons employees leave organizations is because they do not feel valued. This hurts my heart as I type this statement. How can we not value our people? How can we not love humankind? How can we not value and cherish that which God made in His likeness? Through understanding, we gain meaning. One could also say that mindful is meaningful.

As we grow in deeper understanding of our human experience and our leadership responsibilities, we recognize that we are *meaning-seeking animals*.[5] On a quest as spiritual beings having a human experience, we look for meaning in everything we do and every experience we have.

Many of the clients I coach proclaim to have a challenge with time management. Once we start to explore what this catch-all phrase truly means, we recognize that the time and energy they spend on tasks and meetings have no surface meaning or value for them. Through exploration and deep diving into their reflection zone, we unearth where the hidden meaning lies. Miracles happen when we discover the meaning or reason behind a task. The time spent on or with that task miraculously is no longer an issue. Attaching *meaningful* through the process of *mindful* allows miracles to occur.

Being mindful, and the clarity that comes with it, helps leaders understand and consciously set vision. Working with vision, on purpose, and with intention is covered throughout this text and highlighted in Lesson 4: Intention, and Lesson 8: Passion. We experience incredible focus and vision through the practice of mindfulness.

One of the greatest lessons my father taught me was the ability to see the world through the eyes of an artist. Ever since I could remember, my father has painted. A beautiful artist, he loved everything about art and always has an uncanny sense of seeing the extraordinary in the ordinary. As a child living just outside of Washington, DC, I would spend Saturdays at museums and art galleries with my father. As we looked at a single piece of art for what seemed like endless hours, wondrous miracles occurred. A single brush stroke or subtle color change appeared that I might normally have missed with a casual glance. He pointed out depth, shadowing, and texture. He would find the incredible light caught on an elbow that became an astonishing focal point of the piece. This mindful practice then translated to the vastness of the world around us—to clouds, a single petal on a flower, the joint on a piece of molding, the way the sunrays paint the mountain, or a rickety old barn. My father taught stillness, presence, and living in the moment. He taught mindfulness. He taught beauty.

When we see through the eyes of mindfulness, we are enchanted with seeing extraordinary delights. Reminded of the joyful experiences that await us in mindfulness are the words of Emily Dickinson, "The soul should always stand ajar, ready to welcome the ecstatic experience." Bring it on!

Not only is a mindful practice one that provides clarity, vision, connection, and beauty, but being present in the moment also confers peace of mind. Living in mindfulness is living in peace. This is especially relevant in our current culture plagued with chaos, competition, rage, and fear. Mindfulness is a conduit to an immediate peaceful state, a conduit to conscious contact with God. Gained perspective is one of the many miracles from mindfulness. Awareness, coupled with mindfulness, brings the external and internal into astounding perspective, and boldly stated: *into miraculous manifestation.*

Practice

Mindfulness is not rocket science, nor is it so complicated that you must pay a high price to learn it. Mindfulness is unabashedly simple. Remember, mindfulness is a heightened awareness of what fills your mind. Let's break this down to some simple, basic steps to begin this practice.

Daily

The first step, like awareness, is to stop. This stopping does not require a special chair or pillow. You can stop wherever you are. Just stop.

1. Become aware of what's happening around you, including sights, sounds, and smells.

2. Next, move your body. Notice your limbs, torso, and head. Notice your breathing. Is it shallow or deep? Take a deep breath and let it out very slowly. Do this a couple of times because when you focus on breath, the mind fills with the awareness of breathing, which is a great exercise in uncluttering the mind.

3. You may become aware of thoughts and emotions at this stage. Great! Acknowledge and honor your thoughts or emotions, and then release them. The release may be with words or visualization. Either way is fine. Whichever technique works for you is the right technique.

4. Once you empty your mind, you have a clear space, a clean palate. You choose how you want to fill the space. Do you want to fill it with worry? I recently read a plaque that read: Worrying Is Like Praying for Something You Don't Want. Or, do you want to fill your mind with peace and God?

5. At this stage, you may apply prayer, meditation, affirmations, or simply clean space. You choose. The stillness will bring clarity.

6. If you are new to this practice, you may want to practice each day, starting small with just five minutes at a time. When I first started a daily meditation practice,

I was concerned about the time (yes, time management), so I set the alarm on my phone to remind me
when five minutes were up. As I wanted to add more
time, I would simply adjust the alarm time on my
phone. A funny phenomenon happened; with each
time change on my alarm, my body became so coor-
dinated with my intention that I would conclude my
meditation within seconds before the alarm went off.

Deeper

With time, you may want to build this practice into a meditative
or prayer state for twenty or thirty minutes each day. When you
practice mindfulness in this more formal state, miracles occur
throughout your day in extraordinarily ordinary ways. Warning:
you may wonder where all of these butterflies used to live or
for the first time see a breathtaking sunset worthy of a photo in
a magazine!

At Your Desk

You may go into mindfulness anytime, anywhere. I often close my
eyes at my desk and stop when I feel overwhelmed. I'll take a
few deep breaths and clear my mind. After a couple of moments,
I am ready to go back to work, armed with clarity and focus. I
am reminded of this beautiful statement found in Psalms, *Be
still and know that I am God.*

Pause

You are now invited to pray, reflect, or meditate on . . .

Dear God,

You have blessed me

with my mind,

a gift and not a curse.

Help me explore

the depths of my mind

to reach you

and know that you are God.

I pray with a hope-filled

and joy-filled heart

to be mind-filled

with your wonder

and to see the extraordinary

in the ordinary.

I thank you

for the beauty that surrounds me,

even that which I do not yet see.

Amen.

3
LESSON

INTUITION

The intuitive mind is a sacred gift and the rational mind is a faithful servant. We have created a society that honors the servant and has forgotten the gift.

—Albert Einstein

Teachings, Thoughts, and Theories

Western culture loves proof, anything empirical that has evidential credibility attached to it. I'll never forget an experience I had early in my corporate career. One of the first meetings I had in my new position leading the marketing division was with the company president. I was excited with nervous anticipation. Having done my homework in the area of our planned discussion, I felt that I was ready. The meeting began smoothly, and I felt confident in my knowledge and insight. Then, my moment came. The president asked me about my thoughts. I promptly answered, "I feel . . ." and immediately was interrupted by him with a hand to my face and words that cut to my core, "Maria, I don't care about your feelings, tell me what you *know*."

That experience was one of the first of many that unfortunately taught me how to *not* listen to my intuition. Enter *spreadsheets* (the language of corporate America). Luckily, I only followed this mode of operation for a few years, before I realized that my previous way of decision making—using my *intuition*—served me much more efficiently and effectively. Funny thing about the corporate environment—if you can prove something on a spreadsheet, you have instantaneous credibility. Therefore, I quickly mastered the art of gathering empirical evidence to prove what my intuitive mind already knew.

I shudder to think of all the wasted hours I spent looking for evidence to support my feelings. My company was once getting ready to release beautiful custom lots for sale and they needed pricing. I asked our sales agents to go out, look at the lots, and come back with their recommendations. Shortly after that, our general manager, the director of development, and I (the three highest paid senior leaders in our organization) walked each of the four-acre lots, armed with a spreadsheet and a complex formula for determining the prices. This process took nearly three days. Just for fun, I wrote down the price I thought each lot was worth, which I had determined within the first five to ten minutes at each site based on my intuition. When we completed this exercise, my prices were different from the formulaic ones, and to my delight, closely aligned with the sales team's recommendations. After another day of entering our data into the spreadsheet to calculate the ratings, the prices were so far out of line that the sales team nearly mutinied! Needless to say, the approved prices ended up much more aligned with my intuitive prices, several days and thousands of dollars later.

I am not advocating throwing logic out the window. What I am advocating for is a holistic use of all the divine gifts bestowed upon us. Logic is but one of the effective tools available to leaders. A combination of both sensory awareness and intuitive awareness is a powerful force. Intuition is like a *thinking feeling*—a *thinking gut*. This *thinking* assists us in our fast-paced world to make quick decisions with confidence and accuracy.

> **A combination of both sensory awareness and intuitive awareness is a powerful force.**

Leaders successfully use intuition but then can be hesitant to disclose that they used it. I conducted a study on decision making and leadership where I interviewed a high-level hospital administrator who claimed to use intuition effectively in her decision making. However, she informed me that she would never dream of openly discussing her use of intuition with her peers. She said, "In my understanding of the business world . . .

it may be a dirty little secret." Let's bring this powerful, innate part of our authentic selves out in the open with no need to keep it a "secret"—dirty or otherwise.

In Plato's discourse, *Meno*, he wrote, "And if the truth of all things always exists in the soul, then the soul is immortal. Wherefore be of good cheer and try to discover by recollection what you do not now know, or rather what you do not remember." *Soul knowledge*, as Plato wrote, is when we know something, *really* know something, deep down in our heart. We know that *something* to be true, to be real. Intuition comes from this interior place of knowing. When we tap into our intuition, we are tapping into our soul. Our soul knowledge, or intuition, is a deep knowing in our hearts. A participant in my study referred to intuition as "evidence of one's soul." Plato would agree.

In *Mindfulness for Beginners*, Jon Kabat-Zinn wrote about the Buddhist teaching of our "sixth sense." This sense includes the mind; however, the Buddhists don't mean *thinking*, they mean *awareness* and the capacity of the mind that knows things non-conceptually. Frances Vaughan wrote, in *Awakening Intuition*, "Self-awareness is the ground from which intuition comes to full fruition."[6] She describes four distinct levels of intuitive awareness: physical, emotional, mental, and spiritual. The physical level is when we know without knowing, often referred to as a *gut* feeling. Sometimes people refer to this physical reaction of intuition as *instinct*. Being in tune to our body signals is a great way to develop this level.

On an emotional level, intuitive awareness comes through feelings. When we meet someone for the first time and we immediately like or dislike them, even before he or she opens their mouth, it could be our intuitive emotional insight kicking in. We try to describe this phenomenon by stating this person was putting off good or bad vibes. Our intuition responds to this vibration energy.

At the mental level, our intuitive awareness manifests itself through images and clarity. This is when we quiet the mind and come into a fuller level of awareness. You may have had the experience of waking up in the middle of the night with the answer to a problem you were not able to solve during your waking hours. This is a demonstration of mental intuition in full swing as the great puzzle solver. With mental intuitive awareness, we solve patterns, decode chaos, and move out of uncertainty. Management and leadership expert Henry Mintzberg advocated for development of both the right- and the left-brain hemispheres, effectively rendering managers and leaders more adept at making decisions. He recognized the importance of combining both logic and intuitive forces into the power of a holistic approach.

Spiritual intuition, as Frances Vaughan explains, is pure or even mystical in nature due to the distinct independence of senses, feelings, or thoughts. This level of intuitive awareness is a holistic perception, transcending the egoic or rational processes. The practices of mindfulness and meditation tap into this level of pure intuition. With practice, and with relearning how to recognize and leverage intuition, leaders may use this force with tremendous success.

Impediments to intuition come from egoic sources such as fear and selfish desire. We experience these blocks when our minds are filled with worry, doubt, fear, and envy. We claim to not be able to "think straight" in these types of situations. That is because we are not in our *right mind*; we are in the insanity of ego. Recognizing this blockage and consciously making contact with Spirit can right our minds and put us back in touch with our higher self, our intuitive flow, the Holy Spirit.

The incredible use of intuition assists leaders in making rapid decisions with confidence and success. Intuitive leaders are innovative leaders. They are the ones unencumbered by overthinking and who have a feeling for what may be needed. By tapping into our inner knowing, our intuition becomes a perception decipherer, without judgment, and works quickly with precision. We simply need to learn to get out of the way. We get in the way when we try to rationalize our intuitive decisions, cluttering the decision process and adding unneeded complexity.

Many of us must relearn our intuitive wiring. The great news is that intuition never leaves us; it only goes dormant when we stop using it.

Practice
Nine Steps to INTUITION

Intuition development is easy to remember with the acronym, INTUITION. Practice these steps regularly and you'll be on your way to intuitive insight.

Imagery – Exercises in imagery allow the intuitive mind to use the images and symbols of the right brain. The left brain is primarily where the logical, rational thought process occurs. We have a well-developed left-brain process because of our Western cultural teachings. We need to develop the use of our right-brain functions, and imagery aids help us in this development.

Imagery is a powerful tool for many different situations.

I worked with a client who had disturbing images in her head from a movie she had watched. The unsettling images gave her nightmares and started affecting her daily concentration at work. I walked her through an exercise of imagining opening her head like a lid on a hinged chest, and then reaching in and taking out the disturbing images. She then imagined putting the images on a piece of paper and, in her mind's eye, lighting the paper on fire. As she watched the paper burn to ashes in her imagination, she knew the disturbing images were gone for good. Storytellers are masters with imagery.

Non-judgment is the next step in intuitive development. Suspending judgment on your thoughts and feelings is critical to this practice. Honor and recognize the flashes of knowing that come from the intuitive mind. Suspending judgment is one of the most challenging activities for the ego. The ego exists to separate, and judgment is one of the fastest ways toward separation. Remember that God is love, and anything that does not come from love comes from fear or ego.

Thankfulness is a powerful filler for the mind. You will see that while practicing gratitude and thankfulness, God answers, "*You are welcome*" and presents yet another gift. Gratitude is the portal through which abundance flows. Exercises I've personally used and that I utilize with my clients always bring about miraculous results. In my journal, I like to record at least five things for which I am grateful each day. The five things may be people, events (such as the incredible sunset my husband and I watched this evening), or material items such as your home. The point is to take the time each day to stop and reflect on the abundance already in your life, your full life, where nothing is lacking.

When we focus on what we lack, we get more *lack*. When we focus on the abundance, that is exactly what we receive—an abundant flow. If journaling is not your thing, you may want to use a gratitude board. Our gratitude board at home is a chalkboard stocked with different colors of chalk. We invite family and friends to add to the board, and we simply write something for which we are grateful in that moment. I remember after a terrible storm before Christmas when our daughter was coming home for the holidays. Her drive took five hours instead of the usual three because the rain and blowing dust from the storm became mud so thick that she had to creep along at a snail's pace. The moment she walked in the door, before the customary hugs, she dropped her suitcase and went straight to the gratitude board, thankful for making it home safely.

Uncomplicated thoughts are intuitive thoughts. Remember while reconnecting with your intuition that the intuitive mind is uncomplicated and brief. The logical mind is long-winded! We have a tendency to want to complicate the way we work, and I've yet to understand the reasons why. Perhaps it is the ego's way to push us farther away from our Source.

Impressions – First impressions are usually correct intuitive guidance. The emphasis here is on *first*—the very first reaction, not the one that immediately follows in judgment. Remember the gut reaction discussed earlier? We get this unexplained immediate response when we meet someone or go somewhere that resonates, for instance, *danger*.

On a vacation to visit some friends, we failed to make hotel reservations, thinking it would not be a problem that time of year. Unfortunately, we were wrong since our trip coincided with a big festival in the town we were visiting, and we could not find a hotel room anywhere.

Finally, we found a room at an inexpensive motel in an undesirable location. The moment we pulled into the parking lot, I was on high alert. Something just didn't feel right to me about this place. We got into the room right after the housekeeping staff had left, which gave me a minute level of comfort since at least the room was clean. We rationalized the decision to stay, telling each other that we were only sleeping there and spending most of our time with our friends.

I decided to take a shower and freshen up before we went out. Unfortunately, our "clean" tub was so slick my husband had to hold me up so I wouldn't fall! I then proceeded to dry myself off with a towel you could see through. When I got out of the bathroom, I noticed I could see light through a one-inch gap under the front door.

After we got ready, I felt more and more uncomfortable with this lodging choice, and my intuition kept telling me to leave. I told my husband how uncomfortable I felt, and he thought my reaction was simply travel stress and hunger, thinking I would feel better after dinner.

As my husband and I were sitting on the bed, getting ready to go out for the evening, a man with wild hair, crazy eyes, and a wad full of cash in his hand knocked on our motel room window. We all looked at each other, and the man quickly said, "Sorry, wrong room!" My husband looked at me and said, "Ready? We're outta here!" and within two seconds, we checked out of the room. I felt instant relief as we drove away. Later that evening, as we passed by that same motel, we saw a half-dozen police cars and crime scene tape blocking the parking lot. My husband has never doubted my intuition since.

Time – Take time to relax and quiet the mind. Intuition flows more readily in a space free of tension and stress. Another lesson for us to learn in our Western culture is to slow down and learn to relax and de-stress. In addition to time management, stress management is another common challenge with my clients. Practicing the exercises in this book will help with reducing stress and making time to relax and quiet the mind.

Instant – Intuitive insight can come to you in an instant. Recognize this phenomenon and do not dismiss it or try to complicate it with rationalization. Learn to be open to those instantaneous insights. Remember that ego is ready, willing, and able to quickly jump in on the heels of immediate insight. Association games and exercises will help to sharpen this skill.

As you practice awareness and mindfulness, this recognition will come much easier for you.

Open – Be open to new insights through free association. Remember to suspend judgment, and challenge yourself not to anticipate a certain outcome. The Pygmalion Effect discussed in Lesson 2: Mindfulness is a powerful phenomenon. Awareness and full presence in the moment will help you be open to insight. When you are aware of an anticipated outcome, acknowledge it, honor it, and then dismiss it. This practice allows your mind to stay open. Miraculous surprises await you when you allow your intuitive mind to take you on this journey.

Namaste – A Sanskrit term used as a salutation, namaste means the reverent honor you have for another person. In other words, to reconnect with your own intuition, learn to honor the soul knowledge of others. Wise leaders know that when they focus on others, they experience deep and profound growth within themselves.

Pause

You are now invited to pray, reflect, or meditate on . . .

Dear God,

Thank you for creating me

with intuitive insight.

I pray that I remain open

to the connection

of the Holy Spirit

and rejoice

in the soul knowledge

bestowed upon me.

Amen.

4
LESSON

INTENTION

Intention is the core of all conscious life.
Conscious intention colors and moves everything.

—**Master Hsing Yun**

INTENTION

Teachings, Thoughts, and Theories

For many of us, intention is motivation, drive, and ambition to succeed. A demonstration of force, determination, or our immutable will to attain or accomplish something indicates that we have a firm intention. This, too, is part of our Western mental model of intention. A deeper understanding of the power of intention, described by Carlos Castaneda, suggests, "In the universe there is an immeasurable, indescribable force which shamans call intent, and absolutely everything that exists in the entire cosmos is attached to intent by a connecting link."[7] This is not a model of perseverance or a mindset where only the fit or determined survive, but a realization of the connection to each other and our Source: God. What this model of intention describes for us as leaders is that we are not alone in the organization, community, country, or even in the universe; but rather, we are linked together to the energetic force of intention.

As we grow in our understanding and appreciation of the significance of intention, we understand when Dr. Wayne Dyer, in *The Power of Intention*, writes, "Imagine that intention is not something you do, but rather a force that exists in the universe as an invisible field of energy . . . It had become clear that accessing the power of intention relieved so much of the seemingly impossible work of striving to fulfill desires by sheer force of will."[8] With openness to this force, the Holy Spirit, we can create the life we want, lead in the direction of our heart, and surround ourselves with people who support us.

> Surrender does not mean the end—it means the *beginning.*

Dr. Dyer describes four steps to intention: discipline, wisdom, love, and surrender. As with any new behavior or task, discipline is necessary in the learning and practice stages. Discipline requires a commitment of the body. The second stage, wisdom, when juxtaposed with discipline, brings together the body and the mind in preparation to call on intention. The third stage, love, combines the body, mind, and heart toward a holistic readiness for intention. Finally, the fourth stage of surrender is kicking ego to the curb and releasing the body and mind from being in charge. Allow yourself to trust in the Holy Spirit to move intention through you in beautiful surrender. Surrender does not mean the end—it means the *beginning*.

Why is intention crucial to our leadership? It is the purpose, the *why* we are here, and our belief in something greater than ourselves; intention is how we derive meaning. To create a vision for our companies, or even our lives, we must first ask *why*? Tapping into the power of intention requires clearing space in our minds, allowing and trusting our intuitive insights to flow.

As stated earlier, one of the primary reasons employees leave organizations is because they say they do not feel valued or fail to find meaning in their work. At a time when the economy started to fail, people were being laid off in vast numbers, and real estate sales fell to nothing, it was not a good time to be in the land development and new home construction industry—which is exactly where I was. Our company was hurting, and the business plan and budgets were bleeding profusely. The organizational culture was abysmal, and employees were wounded and shell-shocked. I went into the general manager's office and suggested we determine how we could help the employees find meaning in their work. His response was, "Meaning is overrated. They should be happy to have jobs." True, they had jobs, and they were probably thankful for that, but they were definitely not happy. It is our responsibility as leaders to find purpose and meaning in what we do, and then translate that meaning to our employees to help them, too, derive meaning, purpose, and value in their work. We spend the majority of our waking hours at work, which alone screams for meaning and intention.

Maslow knew the importance of meaning when he created his well-known and well-respected Hierarchy of Needs theory.[9] The hierarchy model, comprised of five identified need levels, contends that we cannot move to the next higher level until we meet our needs at the current needs level. And we cannot skip levels; each must be met in hierarchical order. The first level, physiological needs, includes the basic needs of food, water, air, sex, shelter, and the avoidance of or relief from pain. From an organizational perspective, we meet our basic needs when we accept a job position. Most people will not even apply for a job if the commensurate pay does not accommodate their basic needs.

The second level, safety needs, indicates that employees must feel safe in order to have that needs level met. Safety, in this case, is both literal and figurative. Of course, if we don't physically feel safe in a place, we usually leave it. It's different at work. Many employees don't feel figuratively safe at work—in other words, they don't trust their employers or organizations. Trust, an element of safety, is in our second needs level and is close to basic, and yet many of us go through our day-to-day lives not trusting each other. Employers often don't trust their employees. We see this demonstrated repeatedly through office policies, time clocks, and in the childlike ways in which adult employees are "led." Why is it that when fully functioning adults enter the doors of organizations, we herd them like sheep or small children? Employees, too, do not trust their employers, keeping documentation files "just in case" they need to do a CYA (cover your assets) move, or secretly planning their escapes to greener pastures. "I can't let my boss know I have this ailment or issue because she will fire me" is too common a sentiment uttered by employees. Trust is one of the top two challenges of 95% of my organizational leader clients. The other one is communication. The two challenges (trust and communication) are intertwined.

Trust is not just a safety need to meet; it is also an essential element to innovation and creativity. In *Knowledge Emergence*, Nonaka and Nishiguchi assert that trust is one of the building blocks for the creation of what they call *ba*.[10] They describe ba "as a platform where knowledge is created, shared, and exploited . . . ba can be spontaneously created, and it can be built intentionally . . . fostering love, care, trust, and commitment among organizational members for the foundation of knowledge creating." Show me an organization that does not want to create and innovate, and I will see an organization that will not survive.

Belongingness is the third level of needs. This level is about our need for connection with other people. We see this need met in organizations when employees start socializing with one another. Socialization may occur at work or going out for lunch or happy hour together. When employees travel for work, even if they are not fond of each other, they often sit together at the conference or at dinner because they want connection and they want belongingness. Even when employees are unhappy with their employer, I have heard them admit that the only reason they stay is because they love the people with whom they work. This is a warning sign for leaders. Once these employees have their belongingness needs met outside of work, they will likely leave the organization.

The fourth level of needs is esteem needs. This is when we desire self-respect, status, and recognition for our accomplishments. "They don't appreciate me around here" is a mantra expressed by too many people. This hierarchical level is a common exit point for many employees. This saddens me, because saying *thank you* has become a lost art in countless organizations. Far too many managers and positional leaders do not feel the need to say thank you because, "That is what the employee is paid to do." Esteem needs do not need to be met with big, fat bonus checks or flashy awards. A genuine and sincere demonstration of appreciation goes a long way. Write a thank-you note, offer praise at a meeting, or send an email to the department acknowledging a job well done, even though "they are getting paid to do it."

The fifth and final level of Maslow's Hierarchy of Needs is the need for self-actualization, the need for meaning. At this level, we have the need for development of our full potential, our purpose. To achieve a sense of fulfillment, we seek to understand, grow, and acquire meaning in our work and in our lives. Again, this is an exit point for many employees who leave their organizations. I recently heard of a phenomenon, the leaking pipeline, where women in mid to upper levels in organizations leave because they do not feel fulfilled and see no opportunities for growth within the company. They have reached a place of un-fulfillment in their organizations and are leaving in droves. Experience, talent, and female role models are exiting the buildings.

The implications for organizations are clear; they have lost a tremendous resource. Sometimes employees are able to stay in their organizations awhile longer if they fill this need with activities outside of work.

While in my corporate position, I simultaneously taught college courses in leadership for over ten years and earned a

Doctor of Management degree in organizational leadership to meet my self-actualization needs. Can you imagine what an organization could gain if the employee's energy and focus was fully engaged in their work, seeking *and* achieving self-actualization? The results would be incredible. As Thoreau would say, "If one advances confidently in the direction of his dreams, and endeavors to live the life which he has imagined, he will meet with a success unexpected in common hours."

In his final book, *The Farther Reaches of Human Nature*, Maslow explained eight behaviors found at the self-actualization level.[11] Those behaviors include sharper concentration, growth choices, self-awareness, honesty, judgment, self-development, peak experiences (aha moments), and lack of ego defense. As a leader, I would love to see these behaviors demonstrated by my team at work, and not walking out the door. Self-actualization is emotional intelligence. Self-actualization is spirituality. Self-actualization is tapping into intention.

We must first derive a clear purpose and support it with intention for a leader to effectively create and sustain vision for themselves and for their teams.

Practice

When my team and I work with organizations on leadership development, we often begin with a values assessment. The following exercises are also located in the companion Action Guide for download at *www.ACourseInLeadership.com*.

Values

Step 1: Identify ten values that are most important to you.

Step 2: Looking at the list of your values, select your top five (in order of importance).

Step 3: Define these five values and the reasons why you find these five values important and meaningful.

Knowing your values helps bring clarity to what is significant to you. Now look at your calendar and review how you spend your time. Do the activities on your calendar align with your values? If not, why? Please take the time to reflect on your response and journal your thoughts.

Mind Mapping

I love the technique of mind mapping and do this exercise with many of my clients. In the center of a clean sheet of paper, write, *"My purpose for living this life is . . ."* and circle it. Now draw lines out from this circle with as many ideas that flow into your head and heart, and draw circles or squares around each one of those words or statements. Always connect the circles or squares with lines to the center circle of your original thought. Below is an example of the beginning of a mind map. What ideas come up for you? Journal any thoughts that come to mind. This activity will help you gain clarity on your purpose and vision.

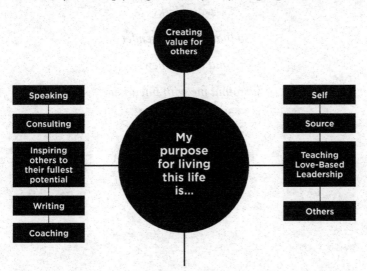

Purpose Statement

Using the above information, write a purpose statement, including the activities involved in achieving that purpose, the people you would think necessary to support you, and the value you provide to others.

I think of the wise words of Thoreau, "If you have built castles in the air, your work need not be lost; that is where they should be. Now put the foundations under them." Or as I say to my clients, "Now it is time to exercise your backbone instead of your wish bone." Harnessing the power of intention to achieve your vision and purpose assures success.

Pause

You are now invited to pray, reflect, or meditate on . . .

Dear God,

I pray that clarity of purpose remains steadfast in my life.

Reveal to me any and all

egoic blocks

so that I may surrender

and begin anew.

Surround me with intention,

light,

and love.

Amen.

5
LESSON

POWER
LISTENING

To listen well is as powerful a means of influence as to talk well and is as essential to all true conversation.

—Chinese Proverb

Teachings, Thoughts, and Theories

Before we dive into the lesson of power listening, I believe we must first review the communication process. Listening is a huge part of communication, and while we have talked in our culture about communication for decades, we still have challenges with effective communication. As I mentioned earlier, trust and communication are the top two challenges of the organizations with which we work. In *Love-Based Leadership: The Model for Leading with Strength, Grace, and Authenticity,* I discuss a study completed by the Society for Human Resource Managers, which surveyed employees who were looking for new jobs outside of their current organization.[12] What is the number-one reason that employees look elsewhere for employment? The reason most often given was lack of open communication. This is mind-boggling. How can it be, after years of emphasis on good communication skills, that we still don't communicate effectively?

Before we beat ourselves up over this one, let's look at exactly what communication is in basic terms.

©2010, Dr. Maria Church International

When we attempt to communicate (as the sender), we tend to forget the *noise* the receiver experiences that interferes with their ability to receive our message. Many factors contribute to this interference, as noise is both literal and figurative. Literally, there are others talking within earshot, traffic outside and in the hallway, computer notifications for new email or social media updates, a meeting reminder, the radio, and a variety of other noises, including the ego. Figuratively, there is the discussion or argument you had at home that morning or the night before, reminder of your child's parent-teacher meeting, the words you exchanged with your boss yesterday, or the report that is due by close of business. All these noises and thoughts going on in our heads are distractions from receiving a message in the manner that the sender intended.

Other contributing obstructions to effective communication are our own mental models, or the ways in which we view the world through our own personal lenses or filters. Built by our life experiences, the location we grew up, religious background, birth order, number of siblings, and education—these factors all contribute to our unique way in which we understand and perceive the world around us. These mental models created throughout our lifetime influence the way we understand events, including communication.

For example, if I were to say "pop," you might think *dad*, a *gun*, or a *soda*. If you hear someone speaking with a certain accent, you may make assumptions about him or her. These are deeply ingrained views that make up our mental models. They are so deeply ingrained that we are usually not even consciously aware of our mental models.

Once we do become aware of our mental models, we can make a conscious choice to change or expand some of our lenses. We can choose to take a step to the left or the right and have a different view, a different perspective, and perhaps a broader perspective. The beauty in all of this is not just to recognize the mental models in ourselves, but also to recognize the mental models of others with whom we communicate. We all have deeply ingrained beliefs that color our world, so the power comes in recognizing these tendencies in ourselves and in others. Can you imagine how much more effective our communication can be with this level of understanding?

How can we know if the receiver understands our message in the manner that we intended? We can ensure that this happens by asking clarifying questions. This requires a reversal of the communication process depicted above. The sender will ask the receiver a question or two to make certain that the understood message matches the intended message. This is a fun exercise and illustrates how everyone communicates in his or her own unique way.

This simple statement, *"I really want to make sure that I am communicating effectively, so would you mind sharing with me what you heard me say to you?"* demonstrates that 1) not only do you care about communicating effectively, but also that 2) you care enough about the other person to make sure they understand. This is a win-win scenario. I have successfully used this technique many times over the years. Each time I use this technique, I am amazed at how differently others heard what I had to say. Nine out of ten times, I must rephrase the intended message to ensure they understand what I attempted to communicate.

Not only do we have the duty as the sender to clarify our message, but also as receivers, we have the responsibility to confirm that our understanding matches the sender's intended message. For example, we could say, *"So what I heard you say is ..."* or *"If I understand correctly ..."* We can do this by simply restating what we believe the sender just said. This practice opens the channels of communication for a more effective and enjoyable experience.

Power listening takes the communication process to a deeper level, one where leaders connect more profoundly with others. Listening is often thought of as a passive activity, which is very different from power listening. Power listening requires action. This deep, active listening means truly showing up for the event—and that event is communication. The active part of listening requires full presence, energy, focus, and utilization of all the senses, including intuition.

As I discussed in Lesson 2: Mindfulness, we can sense when leaders actually show up, versus when only their body does. Showing up requires the leader to be fully present in mind, body, and spirit. This activity requires putting your own needs aside and removing ego from the equation. This selfless act is an exercise in service. Service-based or love-based leadership requires a leader's full presence with their team, being available to them, and being approachable. When we actively listen to others, we honor them with a sacred space of listening. We all have a voice, and we all want to be heard. Just as Maya Angelou said, "I've learned that people will forget what you said, people will forget what you did, but people will never forget how you made them feel."

So much information is available on body language and communication; strategies suggest everything from leaning forward when the other person in speaking, strong eye contact, and nodding your head. All these methods project a superficial sense of being engaged while the other person is talking. Years ago, before I learned about power listening, I became a master at these superficial listening behaviors.

When I came into awareness, I realized how extremely disrespectful I was toward those with whom I had conversations. I would catch myself not listening and have to *fess up*, stating, "I am so very sorry, it looked like I was listening to you, but I was distracted. Would you mind saying it again?" While this statement is what I said aloud, what I was also "saying" is that *I caught myself and you are important to me. I apologize and let's try again.* Leaders are human too. Respect from our team increases when they see us acknowledge our own imperfections and take responsibility for our mistakes.

Full presence requires us to bring our energy right along with us. I recently heard Dr. Jill Bolte Taylor discuss the two types of people on the planet: one gives energy and one takes energy. I would add a third category: one who receives energy. When we are power listening, we are giving *and* receiving energy. When we show up, we are giving energy. With razor-sharp focus on the conversation, we are listening with every sensation available to us. We watch with our eyes, knowing that sometimes our eyes can be deceiving. We also listen with our ears, noticing voice inflection, volume, hesitation, and pace. However, we can also manipulate the use of our voice just like our "listening" body language behavior.

The greatest sense we can use with power listening is intuition, our sixth sense. When we bring our intuition into listening, we bring our energy because we use energy to tap into our intuition. Oddly enough, as we are actively listening, we are also receiving energy. We are tuning in with our heightened sense of awareness—focusing and receiving—which contributes to hearing what both is said and not said in communication. We are aware of the silences, delays, and the energetic feed. I use a variety of mediums for coaching with my clients in person, on the phone, and over Zoom (with or without video). Some of my most profound sessions occur when I cannot physically see my client. I *hear* them more than when I look at them. My senses are heightened, my focus is sharp, and my intuition is in full charge. I hear so much when I cannot see the person.

When we practice power listening, it is vital that we listen without judgment, allowing empathy and love to flow between the two parties. Only then will authentic dialogue occur. When we listen with love, we honor that space for others to have their voice heard. Oftentimes when we speak, we talk aloud to gain clarity. When we actively listen, we generously provide the space. We must stay in a state of awareness, eliminating any type of noise distraction to actively listen. We become mirrors, reflecting back what others are saying, and not saying, without judgment and only with love.

In intention, we find the most important component of active listening—connection with God through the Holy Spirit. Before each coaching session, I begin by tapping into my Source with a prayer something like this:

Thank you, God.

Thank you for the beautiful gift

of service.

I ask that I remain open to your flow,

the flow of the Holy Spirit,

that I may be a channel of

love,

wisdom,

and insight.

Let me hear with your ears.

Let me understand with your heart.

Let me speak with your voice.

Thank you, and amen.

When I coach with full engagement and power listening, I find that questions come up, organically and divinely. I can ask the other person compelling questions, taking us both to a deeper level of communication, meaning, and understanding.

Being fully present and power listening attracts people to you and helps gain commitment from those you lead. I remember reading Dale Carnegie's book, *How to Win Friends and Influence People*, where he described sitting next to a woman at a cocktail party.[13] He engaged her in a few questions, fully listening, and applying the 80/20 rule—listening 80% of the time and talking only 20% of the time. At the end of their chat, she thanked him for the exchange, complimenting him on what a great conversationalist he was! We want our voices heard and to be understood.

Practice

In order to power listen effectively with others, we must first step into awareness, including awareness of our own mental models. Once we know ourselves, we need to increase our awareness of our team members' mental models. Be aware that you are entering a conversation, aiming for true connection. Awareness leads to understanding, understanding leads to appreciation, and appreciation leads to acceptance and love. With this newfound understanding, we must be responsible for both sending and receiving information.

> Awareness leads to understanding, understanding leads to appreciation, and appreciation leads to acceptance and love.

Power Listening Four Essential Steps

1. *Be present in the moment.* Show up without hesitation. Turn off all distractions, both literal and figurative, and allow yourself to be focused and tuned into your intuition. Be honest with yourself and others. If now is not a good time to focus on the conversation, reschedule it for a better time. Both you and the person with whom you are talking will appreciate the care in which you are approaching your exchange. A great activity for exercising your power listening and focusing muscle is to count to sixty without your mind wandering. You will quickly become aware of the many internal and external noise distractions. Keep practicing until you reach a count of sixty without your mind wandering. Congratulations, you just achieved a full minute of focus!

   If you do find your mind wandering in a conversation, fess up. Humility is attractive for a leader and shows that we are human. Let's face it; most people appreciate authenticity and truth.

   Practice the above exercise, as well as meditation, and you will find that your mind will wander less frequently.

2. *Remember to suspend judgment when listening.* Do not anticipate what the other person might say, which is an aspect of a wandering mind. If you find yourself interrupting and finishing someone's sentence, chances are you are wandering. Don't beat yourself up should this happen; just keep practicing, and enjoy the process of leadership growth.

3. *Paraphrasing or mirroring what the other person is saying is a good practice for concentration and focus.* Another great benefit of this activity is to confirm your understanding of the intended message. This practice is a good check and balance, ensuring that you are on the right track.

4. *Learn to be comfortable with extended silence.* Think about times when you try to articulate a thought, sometimes saying it aloud for the first time. You may be trying to gain clarity as you are talking through it. When we provide a great listening space, extended silence can be quite powerful, allowing the other person's full thought processes to reach fruition. Our American culture is typically uncomfortable with extended silence, often referring to such pauses as *awkward silence.* However, you are power listening, and there is nothing awkward about giving space and time to someone you care about.

A benefit of practicing the art of power listening is that you become a good listener, translating into an authentic, available, and approachable leader—a leader who shows up.

Pause

You are now invited to pray, reflect, or meditate on . . .

Dear God,

Thank you for the divine gift of listening.

Reveal to me the barriers

of active listening

so I may be fully present

to those with whom I converse.

Fill my heart with your love and light

to channel energy to

and receive energy from

a transference of glorious love.

With profound gratitude,

I thank you.

Amen.

6
LESSON

OPENNESS

Whenever you are tired or weary, seek the Presence of the Golden One, and draw into your Soul His love, His gentle beauty, His refreshment. If you can keep your certain, sure contact with God, nothing can go wrong in your life. You have no need to worry about decisions whether to do this, that or the other. Your decisions will be made for you, but you must be awakened to the spirit, quickened in spirit, so that you will instantly respond to the gentle guidance of the almighty Presence within you.

—White Eagle

Teachings, Thoughts, and Theories

Living with two bulging, herniated discs can be a pain (no pun intended), especially in our rainy season, when my back seems extra sore. During a family barbeque, my sister, who is a registered nurse, noticed that I was uncomfortable and asked if I was experiencing pain. When I asked why she inquired, she said that I looked like I was *guarding*. This is a medical term indicating when a person has pain somewhere in their body; they become rigid as though to protect the area from further pain or injury. We do the same thing in our lives with our minds and hearts. We get rigid and protect ourselves from perceived pain. We guard.

For many of us, to be open means to be vulnerable. We've been open before and we've been wounded. Ego loves it when we stay closed, and it works overtime to ensure that we do not enter openness. "Remember when you did that before and were hurt . . ." is one of the many voices of ego.

Several years ago, I read *Anyway* by Kent M. Keith.[14] He talks about ten paradoxical commandments, all challenging us to remain open, *anyway*. A few of these paradoxes include, "People are illogical, unreasonable, and self-centered. Love them anyway." Anne Frank did. "The good you do today will be forgotten tomorrow. Do good anyway." Mother Teresa did. "The biggest men and women with the biggest ideas can be shot down by the smallest men and women with the smallest minds. Think big anyway." Martin Luther King Jr. did. By the way, Keith's subtitle is *Finding Personal Meaning in a Crazy World*.

When we are open, the gates open to us with divine guidance, to intention, and to the flow of Holy Spirit. Closing the gates of our minds and hearts is insanity. Why do the barriers to openness show up, guarding our sacred spaces? *Ego*, again, is the answer.

Blocks to openness manifest in the forms of negative voices cemented in our dialogue and culture. Evidence of this insanity includes statements like: *Nice guys finish last* or when considering doing something benevolent for someone (a favor): *If you do that for one, you'll have to do it for everyone* or *No good deed goes unpunished.*

Having a closed mind will add nothing but misery to a leader and to an organization.

Today, more than ever, innovation and service are the keys to organizational success. Wise leaders are open to new ideas, new thoughts, and new learning. American scientist and director of the Center for Organizational Learning at the MIT Sloan School of Management, Peter Senge, described, in his book *The Fifth Discipline*,[15] five disciplines necessary for an organization to be in a constant state of learning.

The first step, personal mastery, requires an individual commitment to be open, stretching one's self outside of his or her comfort zone, learning, and growing. Mental models, Senge's second necessary discipline, which I described in Lesson 5: Power Listening, is an understanding and openness to other perspectives. Shared vision, the third discipline, requires cooperation in the direction forward, being open to a collective vision, and not just the leader's way. The fourth discipline of team learning is crucial for organizations to survive and thrive through innovation, reimagination, and reinvention. The final discipline, systems thinking, opens one's perspective to see the big picture and how the entire system functions instead of narrowly focusing on one's own corner of the world. Senge understood the value of openness.

Our American culture is extremely averse to risk because the notion of risk implies potential failure. This aversion to risk has paralyzed organizations right into extinction. However, those leaders who are not afraid of risk or failure have experienced success far beyond their imaginations. Leaders such as Steve Jobs, Elon Musk, and Bill Gates are constantly innovating and open to new ideas—knowing that some will be successful and some may be failures. Sir Richard Branson, founder of the Virgin empire and one of the most successful entrepreneurs of our time, is not afraid of failure—and he has failed many times. The openness, fearlessness, and love of what these leaders do has made their organizations hugely successful.

We often close our hearts to love, and not just romantic love. We seek to keep a professional distance from the people with whom we work. The irony of this practice is that we spend more time with our coworkers than we do with our friends and family at home.

I coach and consult with several female executives who desire to relearn how to be warm and approachable at work. Many professional women did not have female role models early on, so we modeled the behavior of our male counterparts. I am not implying that men are cold; we know that men and women respond differently to situations and to people. Typically, women are more nurturing, and men are more competitive and aggressive. Notice that I say *typically* because we acquire additional skills with our leadership development and growth. The challenge for women in executive positions is that the behaviors modeled are not authentic for women to adopt. Don't get me wrong; we learn them and we move up the ladder. The key word here is *authentic*. Aggression and competition may not be the right fit for a woman who values nurturing and collaboration.

To be open, we must surrender our plan for God's plan, our will for God's will. Author Marianne Williamson described this process as picturing a file, and the file name is *God's Will.*[16] We can work on the computer all day, but if we do not download the file and open it (our free will), it is just a file. This doesn't mean the file is nonexistent if we don't open it. It doesn't go away; it stays there, unopened. We need to be open to the download and then to surrender to the glory of God.

We don't open the file for a variety of reasons, all of which involve the ego. *I know what I want for my life, and I am going to get it!* This statement is reminiscent of a two-year-old stomping her feet, fists clenched, red face scrunched, preparing for a full-on tantrum until she gets her way.

Why do we get in our own way? Could it be that we think we can plan our lives better than God can or that God won't understand the ins and outs of our organization? The implication is that God couldn't possibly understand the dynamics of our relationships. Now *that* is insanity.

To be open, we need to slow down. To receive, we must be open. We get so busy planning and maneuvering the pieces of our lives, steeped in fear, worry, and anxiety, closed to any divine flow, that we miss the very thing we seek—love and a life open to the possible.

I recently coached a young woman seeking clarity in her life. In her midtwenties, she felt pressure from her parents as well as her own self-imposed pressure to find a "big-girl" job because her peers were settling down with their careers and marriages. She said, "The weight of having to do something awesome, to do great things, to change the world, is too much. Why can't we just come into the place of contentment in our minds no matter what we are doing? What I want for my life is meaning: meaningful relationships, loving God, and loving people." That realization and articulation was like a wake-up call for her. She realized that to live a "great life" meant to develop meaning relationships with God and others—whatever she chose to do and wherever she chose to work. She gave herself permission to "not do great things" and discovered that the simplicity of her desires *was* something great. She became a leader in that moment —a leader of her life as she opened up and surrendered to the divine flow of Holy Spirit. With the pressure lifted to do "great things," she found a job she enjoyed doing with people she en-joyed being with. Her relationship to God deepened, and she had extra time to do volunteer work that was meaningful to her. She found happiness and contentment in her surrender.

Opening our perceptions and inviting in the Holy Spirit through surrender allows healing of the mind and heart to take place. Through healing, the ego no longer erects barriers and blocks to the gates of openness. Just as a clenched fist cannot receive a gift, a closed mind cannot grow, and a closed heart cannot receive love. The conduits to an open heart are kindness, love, care, empathy, and compassion.

> Just as a clenched fist cannot receive a gift, a closed mind cannot grow, and a closed heart cannot receive love.

I was once a senior leader in an organization where a colleague of mine—another senior-level execu-tive—and the company president parted ways in a heated exchange. Their relationship had dete-riorated over time and ultimately ended in a firestorm of angry words. The behavior on both parts was an unrehearsed acting out of wounded feelings, resulting in hurtful expressions of an-ger and bitterness toward each other. In a private meeting I had with the president, where he discussed the anger-fueled event, I agreed that the heated exchange was unprofessional, and I stated that I felt compassion toward the executive who quit. The company president looked at me and asked, "Compassion? What do you mean?" I was floored; he truly did not understand what compassion was or how to demonstrate it. I went on to explain that I wasn't saying the behavior was a good choice, only that I felt love for him as another human being. Even with that explanation, the company president still did not understand the concept of compassion. He only saw that the other person was in the wrong for raising his voice and yelling. In his mind, "wrong was wrong," and there was no room for anything "good" when wrong had occurred. I ended the conversation then, as I realized that we were nowhere near alignment in this discussion and quite possibly in our values. The entire experience caused me to pause and wonder, *How many of us do not understand compassion?* I started to question why I would stay in a job without this alignment. The beginning of the end at that job started for me.

Compassion is giving and receiving love—unconditionally. Compassion is feeling love flow from your soul to another, without caveat. The following teachers, leaders, and mentors describe empathy, compassion, and an open heart so very well:

"When you see yourself in others, it is impossible to hurt anyone else." – The Buddha

"Blessed are the merciful, for they shall be shown mercy." – The Gospel of Mathew

"Seeing Me in all living creatures, know that love for all others is love for Me." –The Bhagavad Gita

"Compassion and mercy bring victory. Heaven belongs to the merciful." – The Tao Te Ching

Practice

Steps in the practice of openness, like the other lessons in this course, first begin with reflection. In what areas of your life do you feel closed or blocked to openness? Work? Love? Spirituality? Take the time now to journal your thoughts. Do not rush through these questions. Sit with your responses and ask yourself why you think those blocks are there.

Q^5 or Five Questions

Ask yourself the following five questions:

1. Is the block to openness true?
2. Is it *really* true?
3. How do I know that it's true?
4. How would I think/act/respond if it were not true?
5. What's stopping me from living my response to the above question #4?

When I go through these five questions with my clients, we rarely move beyond question #2, as the miracle of perception-shifting occurs, allowing them to be open to other possibilities.

RAOK or Random Acts of Kindness

Practice random acts of kindness. These do not need to be grand gestures; sometimes the smaller the better. Try greeting people with a smile, holding the door for someone, or paying the toll for the car behind you on the expressway. Let someone you care about know it with a handwritten note, thanking him or her for being in your life. Give compliments to people you know and to those you don't know. It puts a smile on my face and stirs warmth in my heart when I give a compliment to a server in a restaurant who fixes her hair beautifully and I tell her so. To see the light in her eyes and smile on her face makes my day—and hers. I love win-wins.

Another way to develop compassion is to let go of your need to be right. This was a difficult one for me. Once I tried it on for size, however, it felt good. I felt lighter, almost liberated, like when I earned my first B after a string of As—the pressure was gone. When you give up the stance of always being right, you give up the defense of trying to prove something. Being right is just holding on to a perception. Through changed perceptions, we experience miraculous healing. When you start to feel the need to be right, ask yourself if this is coming from a place of love or a place of ego and fear. Richard Carlson, author of the Don't Sweat the Small Stuff series, agrees, "Choose being kind over being right, and you'll be right every time."

Pause

You are now invited to pray, reflect, or meditate on . . .

Dear God,

You have created me in your likeness,

in love.

Remove all barriers

to my openness

and willingness

to receive your greater good

through the Holy Spirit,

and the channel of your flow

through others.

Fill my mind and heart

with compassion.

May I always be ready and open

to give and receive

love,

knowledge,

wisdom,

and insight.

Amen.

7

PERCEPTION
SHIFTING

If the doors of perception were cleansed,
everything would appear as it is—infinite.
—William Blake

Teachings, Thoughts, and Theories

The group of people lived in darkness inside the cave. Heavy chains bound them to the floor, limiting their mobility. As the fire burned, providing what little comfort they had from the cold, light emanated from the flames, casting shadows inside the cave. Fear gripped them as they watched the shadowy images of the monsters on the walls. A few of the prisoners who escaped the chains, paralyzed with fear, would not step outside of the cave walls because the monster images were too frightening to leave the confines of their dwelling. One day, someone too tired to live in this existence ran from the cave. Blinded by the light at first, it took awhile for his eyes to adjust. As his focus cleared, he saw a new reality: the monsters were not beasts at all; they were human beings, just like him.

Perception shifting is one of the most powerful lessons for leaders. Deeply ingrained in our realities, perceptions are foundational to the way we think, see, believe, understand, and behave in our lives. The power of perception is beautifully illustrated in the story of Plato's cave. The shadows of the people outside the dwelling and the distorted images from the fire flames created a dark reality in the recesses of the cave. What dark reality exists within the confines of the caves of our mind? What distorted perceptions do we hold that may not be true? What perceptions do we have that may interfere with our being the best leaders we can be?

> Choice and thoughts are action movements, directed by us, whether we are conscious of these activities or not.

Perception shifting is one of the most powerful lessons for leaders. Thoughts are powerful; they are the seeds of ideas, beliefs, creativity, attitudes, knowledge, wisdom, and reality. Thoughts can be our best friends or our worst enemies. Not by happenstance do thoughts come to us; these powerful seeds come to us through choice. Choice and thoughts are action movements, directed by us, whether we are conscious of these activities or not. The key lies in awareness of these two incredible gifts—thoughts and choices.

Unconscious thoughts are just as powerful as thoughts steeped in awareness. Earl Nightingale, in *The Strangest Secret*,[17] likened the mind to a fertile field with two planted seeds—one with corn and one with poisonous nightshade. Both seeds, watered and nurtured, grew—because to the field, the type of seeds planted did not matter.

Our behaviors are reflections of our beliefs.

Our minds are the same way, growing whatever our attention plants and nurtures. I saw a sign the other day that stated *Worrying Is Like Praying for Something You Don't Want.* With the continued nurturing and care (attention) given to the seeds of worry, the source of worry will grow and become reality. That is how our minds work; we create our realities.

Negative self-talk is like weeds that have grown in our mind. You know these voices, since many of us have cultivated these beliefs over years and decades:

> *You can't do . . .*

> *You should do . . .*

> *You shouldn't . . .*

> *You're too old . . . too young . . . too fat . . . too thin . . . Who do you think you are?*

Sound familiar? We could probably add to the list with little effort! These voices come from fear, anxiety, doubt, guilt, and shame. Our behaviors are reflections of our beliefs. If we believe the negative self-talk, it manifests in our behavior with ourselves and with others. Do we find that we become stuck, unable to accomplish that goal or unable to overcome our fear of something or someone?

The negative voices and gremlins in our heads fuel underlying beliefs we have about ourselves, others, and the way we view the world. It is important for us to step into awareness and recognize the beliefs that no longer serve us. For example, not talking to strangers is a common lesson taught to many of us as small children. As we grew into adulthood, we abandoned that belief, albeit unconsciously. Beliefs and perceptions are like an iceberg; some perceptions are at the surface and easily identifiable, while other beliefs and perceptions may be deep below the surface. Many of our belief systems and assumptions about the world, others, and ourselves are so deeply ingrained and hidden below the surface that we rarely bring those beliefs to our consciousness. But just because they are not in the forefront of our minds does not mean that they do not exist. In the same way, when a child sits in front of you, covers her eyes, and blissfully exclaims, "You can't see me!"—it doesn't mean we can't see her.

In *Thoughts & Feelings*,[18] Matthew McKay, Martha Davis, and Patrick Fanning identify fifteen key groups of disempowering perspectives:

- Filtering – Focusing on the negative details of a situation and filtering out all positive aspects
- Polarized Thinking – Seeing a situation as either good or bad, right or wrong, perfect or a failure

- Overgeneralization – Making a general conclusion based on a single incident or piece of evidence
- Mind Reading – Making assumptions about what people are feeling, why they are acting as they are, and how they feel about you
- Catastrophizing – Assuming the worst possible outcome will happen
- Personalization – Thinking that everything people do or say is a reaction to you
- Control Fallacy – Thinking that you are responsible for everyone or everything around you
- Fallacy of Fairness – Being resentful because you believe that everything in life should be fair
- Emotional Reasoning – Believing that what you feel is the truth. For example, if you feel unwise, it means that you are unwise
- Fallacy of Change – Believing that you can't be happy unless you can change those around you to behave, believe, or think the way you want them to
- Global Labeling – Generalizing one or two qualities into a negative global judgment
- Blaming – Thinking that someone else causes everything negative in your life
- Shoulds – You keep a list of rules about the way the world should operate and become angry or disappointed if others don't follow your rules
- Being Right – Going to any length to demonstrate your rightness because being wrong is terrible
- Heaven's Reward Fallacy – Feeling bitter when the rewards do not come that you think you deserve after working hard

Perceptions are the stories we tell ourselves regarding what we see and how we interpret the world around us. What are your stories? Do they serve you as you aspire to reach your highest potential? Do your stories lift you up, or do they bring you down? Do your stories represent who you *really* are, your true essence?

Let's look at a possible story: If you greeted someone in the morning at work and he or she did not return your greeting, what would you think? Are they mad at you? Do you wonder all morning what you may have said to tick them off? Do you toss and turn that night because you fear that their lack of friendliness stemmed from when you laughed too loudly at some- **Change your perception and** thing they said two weeks ago **you change your world.** that you thought was a joke, but it turned out it wasn't? Or what if the answer is simply that your coworker didn't return your greeting because they didn't hear you? Alternatively, perhaps they were distracted replaying a discussion they had with their teenager last night. What are the stories you tell yourself? These skewed perceptions sabotage our relationships with others and our relationship with ourself. If your stories no longer resonate with who you are, it is time to create new stories. Change your perception and you change your world.

Our perception of others acts as a mirror of ourselves. What we perceive in others serves to strengthen what we see in ourselves. The attention of what we perceive or notice in other people nurtures what we give attention to in our own minds. If we always see negative aspects of others, we will grow and nurture negative aspects of ourselves. Conversely, if we see beauty around us, we become beautiful. If we see strength in others, we become strong. If we see joy, we become joyful.

The uncomplicated beauty in this lesson is that by standing in awareness and looking at our beliefs and thoughts, we can simply make a choice to keep them or release them.

> **When we release those beliefs and thoughts that no longer serve us, we take back our power from fear to love, from negativity to positivity, from ego to Spirit.**

When we release those beliefs and thoughts that no longer serve us, we take back our power from fear to love, from negativity to positivity, from ego to Spirit. We see and understand perceptions and stand in our power to change those beliefs to experience miraculous shifts in our reality, lives, and work.

Many philosophers, wise teachers, and leaders for centuries have spoken on the power of perception and shifting those realities with conscious awareness:

- Roman Emperor Marcus Aurelius said, "A man's life is what he makes of it."
- The Bible states, "As ye soweth, so shall ye reap."
- To the apostle Mark, Jesus professed, "If thou canst believe, all things are possible to him that believeth."
- Jesus confirmed, "As ye believe, so shall it be done unto you."
- Shakespeare said, "Our doubts are traitors, and make us lose the good we oft might win by fearing to attempt."
- Ralph Waldo Emerson stated, "A man is what he thinks about all day long."
- American philosopher William James confirmed, "The greatest discovery of my generation is that a human being can alter his life by altering his attitudes of mind."

- Dr. Norman Vincent Peale said, "This is one of the greatest laws in the universe . . . one of my, if not my greatest discoveries outside of my relationship to God. The great law briefly and simply stated is that if you think in negative terms, you will get negative results. If you think in positive terms, you will achieve positive results. That is the simple fact, which is the basis of an astonishing law of prosperity and success. In three words: Believe and succeed."

The power of our perceptions and beliefs is not a secret, yet many are not conscious of this incredible law. As I stated in *Love-Based Leadership: The Model for Leading with Strength, Grace, and Authenticity*, "Our willingness to view from a different lens does not imply mastery, only our readiness to change our perception." Perception shifting is one of the most important skills a leader can acquire. Shifting perceptions about yourself, others, and the world around you will change your life. It is that simple, and that profound.

Perception shifting requires awareness (refer to Lesson 1) and choice. Many people believe that they have no choice and that they are victims of circumstance. Leaders must step into awareness and realize that we *always* have a choice. Granted, some choices are more desirable than others, but we always have a choice. Dr. Victor Frankl, former

> We are in possession of these great gifts: to choose our own way and to shift our perceptions from fear to love.

professor of neurology and psychiatry at the University of Vienna Medical School, spent three years at Auschwitz, Dachau, and other concentration camps.[19] Literally and figuratively stripped of everything, Frankl described his experiences, "that everything can be taken from a man but one thing: the last of the human freedoms—to choose one's attitude in any given set of circumstances, to choose one's own way." We are in possession of these great gifts: to choose our own way and to shift our perceptions from fear to love.

Practice

Let's exercise your perception-shifting muscle.

Story Development

In order to begin developing the skill of perception shifting, I like to start with a simple activity to start building our perception-shifting muscle. Find a photo from a magazine. Study the photo and tell a story about it. Make it as rich and deep as you can, developing the characters, setting the scene, and creating the dialogue. Now look at the same photo and create a new story, from a different lens or perspective. Again, develop all of the same elements for a rich, deep story. Practice this activity often to develop your ability to perception shift with ease. This exercise, and my other favorite perception-shifting exercises for you to use with your team, may be downloaded from: https://drmariachurch.com/action-guide-form.

This or That?

Another fun exercise in perception shifting is studying the ambiguous image of the young woman/old woman or the candlestick/faces image. These images and others like them, found online, are fun, easy activities to train your brain to look for more than one perspective.

Five-Times Why

An effective technique for uncovering perspectives that weigh you down is to ask the question *why* at least five times. This process allows you to dig deeper with each response to the question *why*. If you find you are getting some clarity, don't feel you have to stop at five. For example, Ana is late with the sales report.

> *Why? Because she doesn't like to do it* (assumption that Ana has a bad attitude).

> *Why? Because Ana is not good at Excel* (assumption that Ana is looking for an excuse).

> *Why? Because Ana does not want to learn Excel* (assumption that Ana is resistant to change).

> *Why? Because Ana "is not good at numbers" and believes that she is not capable of learning how to work with the numbers* (assumption that Ana is lazy).

> *Why? Because Ana's teacher told her she was "stupid" while trying to learn math.* Aha! Now we have gotten to the root cause of the issue and can address the *real* reason and work from there.

They Saw What?

A powerful activity to practice perception shifting is to think of a situation and look at it from other people's perspectives. Pick three or four people you know and look at the situation from what you believe their perspectives may be. I remember watching a classic episode of the popular 1990's television series *Seinfeld*, where an event happened. The show depicted the event from the four different perspectives of Jerry, Elaine, George, and Kramer. This was a beautiful and humorous example of various perceptions.

What Else Is Possible?

Ask yourself, "What else is possible?" See how many other possible ways you can find to look at a situation. There are always several ways to look at something. Through your brainstorming, possibilities that were not in your conscious mind will surface. Go wild and look at what else is possible.

Remember that perspective shifting requires awareness, choice, and the willingness to be open to other possibilities.

Pause

You are now invited to pray, reflect, or meditate on . . .

Dear God,

I am open to miracles

in my life.

Help me to see the perceptions that stop me

from leading with love

for myself and others.

Open my mind,

eyes,

and heart

to shift my perception

always to love.

Amen.

8
LESSON

PASSION

Above all, be true to yourself, and if you cannot put your heart in it, take yourself out of it.

—Hardy D. Jackson

Teachings, Thoughts, and Theories

We usually include the word *heart* when discussing passion. When we are passionate about something, we often proclaim, *I put my heart into it.* When we want to place emphasis on something, we touch our heart, saying that we *speak from the heart.* This implies a deep core connection, a heart connection. The heart center is the core of our being where passion resides. When we tap into our passion and lead from that space, passion ultimately flows out of every pore in our body. People know it when they see it.

Passion is an attraction magnet. People who enthuse passionate energy draw others to themselves. Because passion is so appealing, it is a great energizing force for leaders. Leveraging passion motivates teams, as passion has motivated the masses throughout history. Passion fueled the migration of Europeans to the New World, the struggle for America's independence from oppression, the movement to secure voting rights for women, the civil rights movement, and the trend toward environmental safety. Passion has taken organizations like Virgin Records, Southwest Airlines, Tom's Shoes, Starbucks, Microsoft, and Apple to unimaginable corporate successes. We see passion demonstrated in great art. Passion is a differentiator. Passion is not complacency or conformity—it is a call to *action.*

Passion is an attraction magnet.

When we think about passion from an individual level, we know we cannot *not* do whatever it is we feel passionate about. Our minds, hearts, and bodies must fulfill the burning desire of passion. To our passion, we say, *yes!* We may be able to put off our thirst for a while, but it burns like a continuous flame inside of us until we extinguish it. The only way to extinguish our passion is to fulfill the destiny inside of us, or we die. Passion must be lived if we are to realize our authentic self.

> Passion drives and motivates us to come into fullness of presence *and* defies time and space through the lasting effects of legacy.

Passion drives and motivates us to come into fullness of presence *and* defies time and space through the lasting effects of legacy.

If you are not sure what you are passionate about, look at your strengths and values (refer to the values exercise in Lesson 4: Intention). There you will find a reflection of your passion. We have developed our strengths, in part because we value those behaviors, and at some level of awareness, we have felt passionate about those activities. With the alignment of our values, strengths, and the flame of passion, leadership effectiveness is certain. This is the road to fulfilling our purpose. Leaders who live and breathe passion inspire others with vision and hope. When leaders have a strong vision, employees and stakeholders are confident in that leader. The confidence of the employees and stakeholders instills within leaders a belief that they will accomplish what they set out to do, thus reaching their full potential.

Vision is one of the necessary skills and duties required of leaders. Creating vision and moving others in the direction of vision is a common denominator in most leadership theories. Whether you lead yourself or others, you cannot lead in a direction you do not know. Vision is a plan of who you want to be and where you want to go. Vision is seeing beyond what *is* and viewing the world in a much larger way.

Finding our vision, and the passion that fuels it, is like finding our voice. Outstanding leaders have passion for their organizations, their people, their causes, and their communities. Leaders realize and care about something much bigger than themselves. Leaders want to make a difference in their lives and in the world. If we have no vision, we do not exist. If we have no passion, we do not exist. Realizing our full potential is living lives in passion and purpose.

Passion is sexy, passion is engaging, and passion is attractive. When I speak to an audience of a few people or to hundreds of people, they feel my passion because passion is contagious. Passion in one person ignites passion in many people, and *there* we connect. Passion is like the eternal flame that lights another wick to keep the fire burning. Passion connects people because we all have the capability of passion. How can leaders inspire passion, motivation, and energy in others if they do not live in that space themselves? True leaders know this, and they readily share their passion and vision with others, exciting them along the way. Passionate leaders know they are part of something bigger, and they invite and ignite others to join them.

When we work with passion, work doesn't feel burdensome. As Confucius said, "Choose work you love, and you will never have to work a day in your life." Our work becomes an extension of who we are when we live in passion. Play becomes work and work becomes play when enveloped in passion.

Many clients with whom I work have a hunger to discover and connect with their passion and, ultimately, with their purpose. The truth is that the connection with passion is really a *re-connection*. Observe a child at play; they are passionate about the activity that occupies their current time. Several lessons come from this observation:

1. Children connect with their passion.

2. They are present in the moment, which helps the passion flow. Their mind is filled with the activity, immersed in the joy it brings them.

3. Children have not yet integrated the negative talk and negative voices into their psyches.

4. They satisfy their need for joy and satisfaction. Passion is the desire to realize and manifest a joy-filled purpose.

Like children, we have the hunger for passion; unfortunately, we have learned to stifle the desire. Instead, we feed the hunger in different ways with substitutes that distract us from our passion and our purpose. Substitutions manifested through this suppression include addictions to work, drugs, alcohol, sex, shopping, and food. When we step into consciousness—understanding, embracing, and fanning the flames of our passion—the need for substitutes will extinguish.

We also need to be aware of passion gone awry. Passion turned into obsession is a dangerous situation for leaders. We have seen passion misused in this way with those extremely effective leaders who captivated followers in both their passion and their vision. Unfortunately, their pas-

What does not come from love, comes from fear. sion and obsession, deeply immersed in the ego, caused mass destruction. Leaders such as Adolph Hitler, Rev. Jim Jones, and David Koresh ignited a shared vision with their followers fueled by obsessive egoic passion. These are examples of cautionary tales whereby passion without love is destructive. What does not come from love, comes from fear.

Passion does not always equate to grand scale. In other words, discovering and harnessing your passion doesn't mean you have to find the cure for cancer, discover an ancient tribe, or invent the next revolutionary device. For some people, that may be their purpose or life destiny. For most of us, finding our passion and bringing it forward may be influencing and teaching our children to realize their greatest potential or creating a painting that touches a person's soul with joy and delight.

For Tom, the cleaning and maintenance man for a home-builder, it meant creating beauty. Tom worked by maintaining and cleaning model homes and guesthouses for potential clients. He treated these houses with great care and love, as if they were his own home. The models and guest homes were so immaculate and clean that if you wanted to, you could eat off the floor in any one of the homes he maintained. Tom passionately cleaned and organized the homes in his care, giving the appearance that the homes had been completed and furnished that day. He delighted prospective customers through all their senses with special hand-selected aromas, fluffed pillows, beautifully folded blankets, and detailed floral and accessory arrangements. Tom was passionate about beauty, and he shared his unique love by ensuring that those around him would experience beautiful sensations as well. The organization led the sales in their market-place, due in large part to Tom's passion.

What entices passion in you? What makes your heart sing, your soul stir, and captivates you for endless hours? Where do you first go in a bookstore? If you had a day off, with nothing to do, what would be your first choice for how to spend your day? What would you teach to others? What brings you joy? The answers to these questions will give you some clues of where your passions lie.

Practice

How do you discover, nurture, and live in your passion? It's not as hard as you may think.

Passion and Purpose Reconnection

Below are eleven steps to discover and reconnect with your passion and purpose. Remember to download the accompanying Action Guide with bonus activities, exercises, and tools at *www.ACourseinLeadership.com*.

1. First, revisit your values so they remain in your consciousness as you proceed through the following steps. Your values are at your core, residing in the same heart center as your passion. In fact, your values will give you big clues about your passion.

2. Identify your strengths as well as those qualities about yourself that you recognize come easily to you. What are your natural abilities? Don't be shy or demure with this activity; identify away.

3. Be open and aware of any emotional or physiological signs from within your body. What excites you or gives you butterflies or tingling in your spine? Often, our passion is trying desperately to come into our consciousness, and our body signals are a great way to move into awareness.

4. Recognize what attracts your attention. Are there certain hobbies or pastimes that you enjoy and look forward to doing? When do you feel most content or happy? Again, be open and aware to recognize how you feel in response to these questions.

5. What inspires and motivates you? Why? Journal your thoughts.

6. As you start to uncover the answers to these questions, be aware of a possible need to seek the approval of others. Be conscious of the fact that you do not need approval to stand in your divinely crafted passion or purpose.

7. Be open to accept and dismiss the disapproval of others. Know that when you align yourself with your life purpose, you align yourself with God. For that, approval from others is not necessary.

8. While moving along in your purpose and vision, don't focus on the outcomes, as the outcomes may look different from what you anticipated. The detachment from outcomes allows you to flow with the present and remain open to the possibilities of divinity. This practice allows you to enjoy the journey and not just the destination.

9. Like the well-known Nike advertisements say—*just do it!* Don't pass from this life with your purpose still in you. Our purpose involves sharing our God-given will with others—*always!* Through service, we realize passion, happiness, purpose, and joy.

10. Remember that when we surrender, we begin anew. With the realization of our passion, we surrender to its glorious divine order. The divine order is of God, and we need to remind ourselves that God's time is not necessarily on our schedule. When we surrender, we let go of the egoic need to control every detail. Believe that God can handle it.

11. You do not have to leap into passion all at once. Take
baby steps to live in passion. Soon enough you will
find the natural, authentic way to step into passion
with full abandonment and still survive in this world.
In fact, you will not only survive, you will thrive when
you step fully into passion.

Pause

You are now invited to pray, reflect, or meditate on . . . .

Dear God,

Ignite the fire of passion in my heart that I may realize my purpose
in service to others.

Through love,

in love,

and for love,

may I lead with passion

and purpose

to fulfill my destiny.

Amen.

9

LESSON

GRATITUDE

When you are grateful, fear disappears and abundance appears.

—Anthony Robbins

Teachings, Thoughts, and Theories

I love the phrase "*an attitude of gratitude.*" What exactly is an attitude of gratitude? In basic terms, gratitude is thankfulness. We usually remember to give thanks in those times when we feel great. However, living in a state of gratitude is much like living in a state of awareness; it is a way of *being.* Gratitude may be an activity, but you will live a much fuller life and lead others more effectively if it becomes your natural state and not simply an occasional activity.

I'm not just talking puppies, kittens, rainbows, and rose-colored glasses. It is to your advantage to practice gratitude. Think of it as a *best practice.* Several studies conducted by Dr. Robert Emmons and Dr. Michael McCullough extol the benefits of a grateful mind and heart.[20] One of the studies concluded that the regular daily practice of gratitude increased happiness by 25%. Emmons also found in a separate study that patients with debilitating health conditions slept better and were optimistic about their life when they focused on gratitude. These studies reflect the fact that grateful people report higher levels of alertness, enthusiasm, determination, optimism, energy, health, wellness, and love.

> It does not matter if you are thinking scarcity or abundance; it will become your reality.

In addition to the health benefits of gratitude, it is also an abundance magnet. The power of attraction applies—abundance creates more abundance. The challenge with *abundance thinking* is the scarcity cycle in which many of us have found ourselves. Let's face it, from childhood we learn scarcity. Scarcity thinking is focusing on lacking such things as finances, health, relationships, opportunities, and so on. The important fact is remembering that whatever we focus our thoughts and attention on becomes our intention, and the universe conspires to manifest that energy into reality. It does not matter if you are thinking scarcity or abundance; it will become your reality.

Sometimes scarcity thinking shows up in the form of accumulation and greed; *I have to get, get, get, and keep, keep, keep.* People who tend to hoard experience deeply immersed beliefs of scarcity mental models. Both the fear of letting go and the fear of surrender block love, abundance, and joy from flowing in our lives. If we hold on to something—*anything*—too tightly, our hands cannot be open to what may be coming. We focus on doing instead of being, on getting instead of giving, and on differences instead of commonalities.

Sometimes we fear a perception of vulnerability attached to gratitude giving. We fear that if we are free flowing with our appreciation to someone that we may be *taken advantage of* or give *too much* and not get anything in return. The downside of this scarcity mental model is that in withholding the flow of gratitude, appreciation, and love, the person will receive more of: a withholding of gratitude, appreciation, and love. See how this works?

Gratitude is the portal through which abundance flows.

Gratitude is one of the highest forms and expressions of love. The more freely we give it away, the more freely love and abundance flow to us. This is a simple concept; no need to make it complex. Gratitude is the portal through which abundance flows. Cultivating and sharing gratitude is an immediate way to shift the energy and start the flow. Think of a time when you gave someone a compliment or showed appreciation for something he or she said or did. Do you remember how they perked up? The energy shifted the moment you shared appreciation.

Acknowledgment is also a great conduit for practicing gratitude. It is important to acknowledge ourselves for accomplishing what we intended. Too often, we check the box *done* and move on. Stop. Acknowledge. Celebrate. Again, this demonstration of appreciation shifts our energy. We bring gratitude to our consciousness through appreciation, and we attract more because of the shift in our energy.

Acknowledge others, too. Seeing the good in others is not looking through rose-colored glasses; it is a miracle in shifted perception. Remember, abundance attracts more abundance, negativity attracts more negativity, and good attracts more good. When we focus on the good in others, we give them the benefit of the doubt. With love, leadership, encouragement, and guidance, we can work on what's right instead of focusing on what's wrong.

Renowned psychologist B. F. Skinner knew this concept and framed it under the teachings of behavior modification.[21] He knew that reinforced behavior would bring about more of the same behavior. I have used this practice for decades in the workplace, with great results. Acknowledging someone for a job well done, a beautiful blouse, the way they fixed their hair, expert sales skills, the warmth with which they answered the phone, or the way they organized their office are all outward expressions of sharing love, gratitude, and value with others.

Living in a state of gratitude is living in a state of intense joy. Gratitude is deeper than happiness; it is a profound state of joy-filled contentment. This is a state of authentic awareness. We see beauty around us, in big things and in small, and do not take things for granted. We may rejoice in a variety of abundant, endless gifts:

- A smile
- A beautiful sunset
- A lizard doing push-ups on the wall
- A butterfly fluttering from flower to flower
- Children playing
- Sunrays penetrating the skyline
- Laughter
- Raindrops
- The fresh smell of clean sheets
- Holding an old book
- Opening a new book for the first time with the eagerness of a child on Christmas morning
- A roaring fire in the fireplace on a cold winter night
- Holding hands
- And the list could go on and on.

This is the joy of living in abundance—the joy of living in a state of gratitude.

Generosity is also an offshoot of living in gratitude. The moment we step into awareness of abundance in our lives, we become acutely mindful of sharing our gratitude with others in the form of generosity. I am not only talking about giving gifts or donating to charity, although that is certainly a form of generosity. I am also talking about giving to others our time, attention, love, thoughts, and care.

The moment we step into awareness of abundance in our lives, we become acutely mindful of sharing our gratitude with others in the form of generosity.

I remember those times in the office when we were stressed and worn out from trying to meet incredibly tight deadlines. The look of near exhaustion from the staff in the final stretch told me my team was near their breaking point. In those times I would stop, go to them, sit, and simply be present. The straightforward act of care and appreciation worked wonders—in the form of renewed energy, lifted spirits, and increased joy.

I am forever grateful to Dot, a professional volunteer forty years my senior, for teaching me an important lesson in my early twenties. I met her and a handful of volunteers at a large event we were organizing. It was early evening with all the promise of a very late night. I left our six-year-old daughter at home with my husband, and she told me tearfully as I left that she never got to see me. I was still reeling from that heart-wrenching encounter when I arrived at the venue. Sharing the story with Dot about how bad I felt and expecting some sympathy, she surprised me by sternly telling me, "You should feel bad. She's your daughter, and she comes first." *Wow*, that hit me right between my eyes. I immediately returned home to the open, loving arms of my daughter, learning the importance of giving time generously and with love. Thank you, Dot.

What happens when we experience challenging times in our lives, when it seems like there is nothing for which to be grateful? Ah, those are what I call *seat-stirring* moments, those moments when we experience great learning. During our challenging times is when we can experience miracles. Shifts in perception are the power tools of the Holy Spirit. To shift, we first start by reflecting on those experiences, listing what we have learned. This activity will help frame and identify those elements for which we are grateful. The same process goes for relationships—looking for the lessons learned and for the good in the person or the situation. Challenges train us to look for those positive elements, even during turmoil. Remember to stay focused on love and not succumb to fearful thoughts.

Practice
Gratitude Journal

I remember reading an article about gratitude several years ago. The author talked about keeping a gratitude journal. This idea intrigued me, and I decided to commit to keeping this journal for a full year. Each day I listed at least five things for which I was grateful, no matter how big or small. Some days the list was a dozen, and other days I struggled to come up with five. Then something happened. I soon realized that wherever I was grateful for something, I began to receive more of it. Abundance did indeed flow. Blessings surrounded me in my life and my work; my health, my pastimes, and love became much more rewarding than ever before. To this day, I still reflect on gratitude in my journal and continue to be blessed beyond belief. Keeping a gratitude journal has also enhanced the lives of many of my clients.

Some questions I like to use with clients for journaling exercises follow:

▶ For what are you grateful in this moment? This hour? This day? This week? This month? This year?

▶ What attitudes and behaviors did you do today to demonstrate gratitude? How did it feel? Describe those elements.

▶ Is gratitude one of your values? Why or why not?

Daily List

An extension activity to the gratitude journal is to look at your daily list of gratitude items and write down what you did to receive those gifts. For instance, you are grateful for your home; what did you do to realize that home? For the beautiful sunset, what did you need to do to receive the sunset? Probably it took presence and stillness to receive the splendor of the sunset, not taking it for granted. By identifying what you did to receive the blessings, you become aware of your power over your thoughts, attitudes, and behaviors. This awareness reinforces the amazing power of choice in your life.

Gratitude Board

A fun activity many of my clients participate in is posting a gratitude board in a prominent place in the home. This could be a chalkboard or a white board. List anything on the board for which you are grateful, and invite family and friends to participate too. The board serves as a visual reminder each time you pass by it. I described how my family uses this board in Lesson 3: Intuition. Writing on the board and practicing gratitude has become an integral thread in our family.

A Letter a Day Keeps the Blues Away

Another activity to cultivate gratitude in your life is to write a letter a day for one year to different people, indicating why you are grateful for him or her. This activity is beneficial to so many people on numerous levels. Your generosity will move and touch the hearts of all the people who receive letters from you. You, too, will receive joy and love in your heart all the while you are writing the letter, shifting your energy to love each day while you are thinking about that person and completing the activity. Finally, what you sow, so shall you reap. Happy harvesting!

Pause

You are now invited to pray, reflect, or meditate on . . .

Dear God,

I thank you for the many

Joys in my life.

The warmth of the sun on my face.

The love swelling in my heart.

I pray that I may see

the obstacles to

gratitude,

joy,

and abundance;

and remain open

to receive the holy gifts

from you.

May I always remember

to pass them on to others

with the same joyful heart

in which I receive

your splendor.

Amen.

10
LESSON

GRACE

Everybody can be great . . . because anybody can serve. You don't have to have a college degree to serve. You don't have to make your subject and verb agree to serve. You only need a heart full of grace. A soul generated by love.
—Rev. Dr. Martin Luther King Jr.

Teachings, Thoughts, and Theories

Why would *grace* be included in a lesson on leadership? How can it not be? Grace is the state many wise leaders seek—*grace under fire*. The state of grace, however, is not just essential under fire; grace serves leaders all the time. During times of stress, confusion, joy, and peace is when grace is at its best.

Many leadership books talk about policies, procedures, and processes. The extreme challenge in today's organizations is that we often value policies and procedures more than we value and honor people. As the Rev. Dr. Martin Luther King Jr. said, "We need a heart full of grace." Found in love, grace personifies elegance, politeness, and generosity of spirit. An organization steeped in love is an organization steeped in grace.

Grace is a concept ripe with different mental models for people. Most definitions and constructs have common elements such as beauty, elegance, dignified manner, generosity of spirit, and a gift from God. The ability to see beauty in *anything* is a gift of grace. Mother Teresa saw beauty in the poorest of the poor when she said, "Each one of them is Jesus in disguise." Grace is seeing with the heart and eyes of God. Victor Frankl described the worst of horrors in his book, *Man's Search for Meaning.*[22] He told a story of sitting on the floor in the concentration camp eating soup, exhausted after laboring all day for the Nazis, when a fellow prisoner rushed in to ask them to join him outside to marvel at the wonderful sunset. Even in the midst of the heinous concentration camps, those prisoners understood the beauty of grace.

Grace is elegance personified. Many of my female executive clients work with me to reclaim their femininity in their high-level leadership positions. Through the process of reconnecting with their feminine energy, they discover elegance and grace. Elegance is refined confidence in self. It is a calm, quiet knowledge of self-efficacy that enables you to handle anything that comes your way with dignity. This comes from knowing that you will *never* run out of resources because you are tapped into your Source, the source of all resources— God. Grace through elegance is a powerful leadership example. I'll never forget when Paula, a colleague twenty years my senior, said to me, "I never knew that a woman could lead with softness and femininity. I always thought you had to be tough, hard-nosed, and aggressive for others to follow. Thank you for showing me another way, an even more effective way—an authentic way." Paula learned the power of elegance and grace in leadership. She saw it, in fact, move mountains.

Grace is elegance personified.

Coming into grace is like coming home to God. Only in a spirit of surrender and acceptance of His divine will shall we find the gift of grace. Through the journey into our inner wilderness, we find our natural state of oneness and solitude with God. This is the call to perception shift from loneliness to *alone solitude*. Through quiet solitude, we discover our natural rhythm that leads to peace, balance, God, and grace. Yrjö Kallinen understood this when he said:

Coming into grace is like coming home to God.

> Grace means more than gifts. In grace, something is transcended, once and for all overcome. Grace happens in spite of something; it happens in spite of separateness and alienation. Grace means that life is once again

united with life, self is reconciled with self. Grace means accepting the abandoned one. Grace transforms fate into a meaningful vocation. It transforms guilt to trust and courage. The word grace has something triumphant in it.

Connecting ourselves with nature is one of the best ways to connect with our natural rhythm. Our natural essence, found in nature, is that of fire, air, water, and earth—in other words, energy, breath, blood, and bones. These natural elements are the physical manifestation of our spiritual essence, our natural essence, the essence of grace. Discovering our essence is unrelated to action but *is* found in solitude. St. Francis of Assisi's wisdom explains this process, "What is it that stands higher than words? Action. What is it that stands higher than action? Silence."

With the full realization of grace, we experience great peace and balance. Happiness and satisfaction emerge in our work and in our lives. Of course, this happiness requires a full surrender of our will to God's will. This statement oftentimes scares people. *Well, what if the will of God is different from my will?* This is not a new fear, as an ancient Chinese proverb states, "Thousands upon thousands of human plans are not equal to one of Heaven's." The resistance to God's will comes from fear. "But," you may protest, "I love teaching and I don't want to be an accountant." If you have a talent for teaching, why would you think that God's will is one where you would crunch numbers? Or a would-be artist *called* to wait tables? God gave you *that* talent and *that* skill to fulfill His will. God gave you grace.

Remember that surrendering to God's will is a beginning. All we really must do is get out of the way. We need to eliminate the noise in our lives and tune into God through the Holy Spirit. Of course, surrender requires openness, trust, faith, stillness, and love. Getting out of the way is opening our mind and heart to the divine directions we receive through the Holy Spirit.

It means movement in the direction of our call, while also not being attached to the outcome. Attachment to the outcome moves us out of the present and away from our divine download. Inspiration (*in-spirit-ation*) comes to us in grace and openness to the will of God.

Our divine quiet grace can shine like an outward beacon. The 3 Cs are the outward manifestations of inward grace: care, compassion, confidence. The confidence comes from our surrender, knowing the powerful hand of God guides us. Confidence is one of the elements that draws followers to great leaders.

Warning: confidence is not *arrogance*. I love the Merriam-Webster definition of arrogance: *an attitude of **superiority** manifested in an overbearing manner or in **presumptuous** claims or **assumptions**.* You will notice that I emphasized all the ego-related words in bold. Yes, arrogance comes from ego, whereas confidence sprouts from authenticity, from grace, from God.

Care and compassion are grace manifested in outward behaviors toward others. Grace, too, manifests through acts of sincere kindness to each other and all living things on earth. Care and compassion are vibrations of love.

Twentieth-century philosopher and theologian Rabbi Heshel described grace under fire when he said, "In every moment something sacred is at stake, and even in that moment of being attacked, something sacred is at stake. Can I choose, or be awake or aware enough to see that going on and to say I need an imaginative, creative, loving response that keeps my power rather than give it over to that person and just act the way they want me to act." Living in that state of imaginative, creative, loving response, as Heshel described, is living in grace. Reclaiming and retaining our power is the power of grace. Martin Luther

King Jr. and Mahatma Gandhi lived in grace, retaining their power while teaching love and peace. Rev. Ed Bacon describes grace manifested as a *unifying breath*. Grace allows us to break the cycle of violence and turmoil and to breathe together as one.

Practice
Right Planning

To begin a practice of tapping into grace requires first surrendering your plans for God's plans. If you are worried about what that may be, recognize the intrusion of ego. When you feel reticent, fearful, or apprehensive, know that is ego is in full swing. God will reveal to you His divine plan of splendor and love divinely designed just for you. The best is yet to come.

Journal Reflection

The following activities for a practice of reconnecting with grace are a series of journal questions. Begin this process in quiet reflection, and call on the ancestors and teachers of wisdom. Here are but a few of those nuggets:

> "If wakefulness is always maintained, then dreams pass away naturally. When the mind ceases to discriminate, all things become as one." —The Buddha

> "In this world you will have trouble. But take heart! I have overcome the world." —The Gospel of John

> "Those who go beyond religion and see Me, the Self, cross over the illusion to Me." —The Bhagavad Gita

> "When he has freed himself and understood hidden knowledge, he crosses over to the other shore. There he will stand on dry land." —The Catukka Nipata Pali Sutra

"The mind which has attained wisdom and peace becomes a mirror of all creation." —Chuang Tzu

"Happiness is the realization of God in the heart. Happiness is the result of praise and thanksgiving, of faith, of acceptance, a quiet, tranquil realization of the love of God. This brings to the soul perfect and indescribable happiness. God is happiness." —Sayings of White Eagle

"If one seeks wisdom, there is no need to leave home." —The Tao Te Ching

"The thing we surrender to becomes our power." —Ernest Holmes

Following are reflective questions for journaling:

▶ To discover your natural essence and rhythm for grace to flourish, reflect on your current relationship with nature. What areas draw your interest: mountains, desert, forest, or water? How do you feel in those places?

▶ What is your mental model of solitude? How do you feel about being alone? What is your relationship with stillness?

▶ How do you live in balance in your life? What keeps you from living a more balanced and grace-filled life?

▶ Currently, what or who is your source of happiness, peace, and satisfaction?

▶ How do you live grace in your leadership? With your friends? With your family?

▶ How do you demonstrate generosity of spirit?

Pause

You are now invited to pray, reflect, or meditate on . . .

Dear God,

I recognize that grace

is not just a prayer before I eat a meal.

Grace is a beautiful, everlasting gift

from you

to me—

an essence,

a state, a way of life.

I surrender to you, Lord,

that I may release any ego

holding me back

from living

a grace-filled life.

I surrender to the beauty

that surrounds me.

I surrender to you

my withholding of a generous spirit,

that I may lovingly share with others

elegance,

care,

compassion,

and confidence.

Amen.

11
LESSON
LAUGHTER

True humor springs not more from the head than from the heart. It is not contempt; its essence is love. It issues not in laughter, but in still smiles, which lie far deeper.
—Thomas Carlyle

Teachings, Thoughts, and Theories

Laughter is completely underrated. Laughter is our heart's outpouring of love. We know laughter is contagious, yet it is powerful medicine. Leadership use of laughter is like a power-charged tool with many uses. One of the most compelling benefits of laughter is shared, joyous connection. Comedian Victor Borge said, "Laughter is the closest distance between two people." He is right; laughter connects us at a deep level, which

Laughter moves beyond the superficiality of words right to our souls, moving all pretense and guard aside.

is why it is so contagious. Laughter moves beyond the superficiality of words right to our souls, moving all pretense and guard aside.

I'm always amazed at the extreme power of laughter, people laughing just in response to someone else's laughter. I remember a time when my husband, daughter, and I were watching a silly movie. The premise was a bit far-fetched, but we liked the actor in the film, Bill Murray. He inherited a circus elephant and wanted to take it across the country to sell it to a zoo. In one scene, he was driving an eighteen-wheeler, which he did not know how to drive, with the elephant in the trailer. In the cab, he had several boxes of candy that he was feeding to the elephant, since he didn't know what else to feed the animal.

As he was driving downhill, he realized his brakes were not working and needed assistance. Another eighteen-wheeler pulled up beside him to give him some help. The other driver was yelling through the window about pulling a lever under his seat. Unfortunately, there were two levers, and Murray's character pulled the wrong one—the one that lifts the cab forward to service the engine. This lever immediately tilted the truck cab forward, to the point that Murray was at a forty-five-degree angle, steering the truck with candy falling forward all over him.

I laughed so hard—it was one of the funniest scenes I had ever seen! Murray was so tenacious trying to steer that rig and appeared calm although he was obviously in bad shape. I can hardly type as I am cracking up reliving the scene. What was even funnier was how hard my husband and daughter were laughing at my reaction. They did not find the scene as hysterical as I did, but my soulful belly laughter was so contagious that all three of us were rolling on the floor in tears. Laughter goes to the core, infecting those within its path.

> **Laughter goes to the core, infecting those within its path.**

Early on in my corporate career, colleagues advised me to learn golf, which they claimed was a great way to network, bond with clients, and create deals. I learned the sport, but I didn't enjoy the game as much as other people did. At one of our corporate retreats, my boss and colleagues couldn't wait to get out on the course with some of the top executive staff. I was a bit confused by this because I knew my boss didn't really get along with this group of people. I asked him about it, and he said, "On the golf course, unless you are a pro, there is no pretense; all are on equal footing and all are hitting poorly." The golf experience allowed them to bring down their guards and share the misery of their poor shots. Like golf, laughter allows us to connect with one another, letting our guards down, sans the misery of poor golf shots.

Laughter enhances communication by letting our shields down and showing that we are human. For too long the model of professionalism has instructed us to be superhuman. We have learned how to work beyond what is humanly possible, denying our natural rhythm for balance. We also have learned to check our emotions at the door. While I ascribe to the concepts of emotional intelligence (EQ), we are still human; we have emotions. To deny that fact is insanity. EQ purports that we understand and acknowledge our emotions, recognize them, and with conscious awareness, not let the emotions rule us. This is certainly a healthy approach to emotions, which is very different from the robotic *professional* corporate model we have learned.

Historically, emotions were a no-no in the workplace; they were something that women had, so they were especially not welcomed in the male-oriented corporate environment. When we learned to suppress our emotions, we learned to suppress *all* of our emotions, including laughter. Because of this emotionless, superhuman, robot-like model that we've been used to, when a leader now brings laughter into the workplace, he or she displays human emotion; and the humanness opens the channels for the leader to connect with others.

> Combating isolation, laughter joins two hearts and two souls together. When we can share laughter with someone, we help lighten his or her load.

Laugher lifts spirits. Many of us walk around with the weight of the world on our shoulders. Connecting with others through laughter allows us to unburden ourselves of the load. Combating isolation, laughter joins two hearts and two souls together. When we can share laughter with someone, we help lighten his or her load.

"A cheerful heart is good medicine," Proverbs tells us. The Koran, too, speaks of laughter, "He, who makes his companions laugh, deserves paradise." Native American wisdom, too, purports that laughter cultivates joy and is good for the heart and soul. Chippewa Larry P. Aitken stated that "laughter is a necessity in life that does not cost much, and the Old Ones say that one of the greatest healing powers in our life is the ability to laugh." Infusing laugher into a heavy situation allows miracles to occur. When we can shift from heavy to light, we experience joy, even in the worst of times. Why do you think we sometimes laugh at *inappropriate* times? It is because our hearts are too heavy, and we need the release. Like a valve releasing pressure, laughter releases burden.

> Like a valve releasing pressure, laughter releases burden.

My colleague Dorothy and I were collaborating on a very intense project with a tight deadline. Focused, we worked diligently and hard. Dorothy asked me a question in a serious tone with deep intensity, interrupting my thinking, and I looked up at her and burst out laughing at the seriousness of our intensity. Deeply immersed by the weight and intensity of our heavy energy, Dorothy, too, folded with laughter—the perfect release for the heaviness we were experiencing. Sometimes we create the weight, especially when we take ourselves too seriously.

I love the story Dr. Wayne Dyer shared in *The Power of Intention*.[23] At an extremely tense meeting, someone was bringing up an issue with anger, and the committee reminded him and other unhappy meeting-goers to remember *Rule #6*. They all would quietly sit back down with this gentle, yet firm reminder. After the meeting, someone asked the committee, *What was Rule #6?*

> Laughter is the skeleton key to any worry-filled door.

The answer—*Don't take yourself so damn seriously!* I immediately made a sign for my desk and look at that reminder when

I start taking myself too seriously. By the way, there were no rules one through five! Once I became aware of those times of taking myself too seriously, I could start laughing at myself. I found out that I am quite funny (to me, that is), and I crack myself up every day. Laughter and the resultant lightness it brings is the key to dispelling worry and burden. Laughter is the skeleton key to any worry-filled door.

Lightness, experienced through laughter, increases optimism. Optimism is a choice to perception shift. Like looking at the cup as half full, optimism allows us to find the positive elements in a burdensome situation. When we experience a cloudy day, we have faith and optimism that the blue sky is just above the clouds. Any of us that have flown in a plane know this to be true. When there is a storm, the pilot flies the plane above the storm clouds to the blue sky. Laughter is the plane that flies us above the worrisome burdens in our lives to the blue sky of optimism. This is not Pollyanna-like thinking; this is as true as the sky is blue. The caveat is we must choose to shift our perception to see it.

Laughter is the plane that flies us above the worrisome burdens in our lives to the blue sky of optimism.

Many studies in medical research extol the health benefits of laughter. Physically, laughter releases endorphins, also known as the *happy hormones*. Laughter relieves stress, lowers blood pressure, and boosts our immune system. In addition to these wonderful physical benefits, laughter lifts spirits emotionally and mentally. Psychologists have used laughter as a method to help people suffering from depression and anxiety. A popular form of this approach, known as laughter therapy, gets people laughing together. Laughter helps us see things more clearly, because it releases the worry, stress, and tension that cloud our thinking.

Tapping into our creativeness is another benefit of laughter, opening the channels of playfulness. By breaking down our external barriers, we may be more prone to be playful, which can lead to creativity and joy. Observe children at play. They immerse themselves in their playfulness and they think of inventive creative concepts and new ways to use toys. I'll never forget the time when Cabbage Patch dolls came on the market. I waited in line before Christmas like thousands of other people to purchase a Cabbage Patch doll for my daughter. I was so excited on Christmas morning and couldn't wait for her to open her "big" present. When she did, feeling my excitement, she too was elated. She promptly tore open the box, pulled the doll out, and tossed her to the floor. My daughter couldn't wait to put the box on her head and walk about like an astronaut in a space suit.

"The human race has only one really effective weapon and that is laughter," proclaimed Mark Twain. Laughter and lightness are great ways to diffuse anger. Twain also said, "Against the assault of laugher nothing can stand." When someone comes at you with anger and conflict, finding common ground is a quick, effective technique. Infuse the common ground with laughter and the confronter's guard comes down, and boom—*connection*. Laughter and lightness can neutralize worry and fear. Let's face it, anger and confrontation spring from fear and worry, and nothing can stand up to the assault of laughter and love.

Smiles are the bridge from seriousness to laughter.

Smiles are the bridge from seriousness to laughter. Have you ever noticed how quickly you can shift energy by smiling at someone? Have you ever felt grumpy and someone smiled at you, immediately lifting your spirits? Smiles are powerful. "A smile starts on the lips, a grin spreads to the eyes, a chuckle comes from the belly; but a good laugh bursts forth from the soul, overflows, and bubbles all around," said author Carolyn

Birmingham. We see the bubbling all around through the contagious nature of laughter.

Laughter neutralizes because it comes from the soul, from God. That is why there is immediate connection because it comes from the place of oneness where we are one with God and one with each other. Laughter is like a wireless network connection to God and to one another—without connection fees. Moving us from the egoic self of separation and super-ficiality, laughter is deep in our souls, born of God's divine love for us. "God is a comedian, playing to an audience too afraid to laugh," [24] Voltaire professed.

Don't be afraid! Fear comes from our ego. We cannot feel more than one emotion at a time, so let's not waste it on worry, fear, or anxiety. Laughter directly connects us to joy and love. These are our divine gifts, not to be wasted. Charlie Chaplin said, "A day without laughter is a day wasted." Let's not waste any more of our time in heaviness, without joy and laughter.

Practice
Laughter Strategies

Here are seven strategies for infusing laughter and lightness in your leadership and life:

 ▶ Start developing your practice of laughter with consciously smiling today. See how many people you can touch and shift their energy with your smile.

 ▶ Begin your meetings on a light note. I have the E*Trade babies' videos on my favorites list and would start meetings with one or two of those commercials. The more I watch them, the funnier they are.

 ▶ Listen to a funny recording in your car on the way to work, setting the tone for the day.

▶ Laugh for 3–5 minutes every day. Fake it 'til you make it!

▶ When you start to feel worried or heavy, ask yourself what is the worst that could happen. Then ask the five questions discussed in Lesson 6: Openness.

▶ What is your funniest memory? Write down all the details, leaving nothing out.

▶ Wear at least one article of clothing or accessory each day that makes you smile, gives you joy, or lifts your spirits. Remember—this can be something that no one else can see (wink, wink).

Pause

You are now invited to pray, reflect, or meditate on . . .

Dear God,

Laughter is the salve

on my worried heart.

I pray that my heart and soul stay open to

the gift of laughter

and the recognition

of ego and pride

trying to get in the way.

May your infusion of

joy in my heart flow out

in laughter,

touching other souls

in my path.

Thank you,

and amen.

12
LESSON
CREATIVITY

*There is no doubt that creativity is the most
important human resource of all. Without
creativity, there would be no progress, and we
would be forever repeating the same patterns.*
—Edward de Bono

*Insanity: doing the same thing over and over
again and expecting different results.*
—Albert Einstein

Teachings, Thoughts, and Theories

Ask any successful leader or business owner to name the most critical factors in success today, and you will hear *innovation* or *creativity* near the top of the list. Now, more than ever, organizations are looking for innovation and creativity skills in their leaders. The old models of leadership, steeped in scientific management and mechanistic thinking, no longer serve our needs in this new era. As Einstein so eloquently reminds us, we must stop the insanity and look toward new models and creative ways of leading people and doing business.

Moving from insanity to our *right* mind is literally working in the right side of our brain. For decades, our American culture has devoted most curriculum and teaching models to developing the left hemisphere of the brain. This is the part of the brain for the logical, linear, and sequential thought processes. This style of learning and development continued into colleges and universities where the mechanistic model of managing business and leading people remained a primary focus. Perhaps a slight nod to the "soft skills" of leadership appeared in the curriculum, but not until quite recently are we teaching these skills to leaders.

Many organizations today focus on teaching the soft skills in their leadership development programs because they have realized a profound need for their leaders to have these skill sets in this new era. The soft skills to which I am referring are connecting with people, motivating teams, inspiring followers, thinking creatively, innovation, quick decision making, and big-picture vision (strategic thinking and planning). Each one of these skill sets requires right-brain thinking.

Daniel Pink described the differences between the right and left hemispheres of the brain in his book *A Whole New Mind*.[25] The left hemisphere, which controls the right side of the body, is sequential, specializes in text, and analyzes details. These skills probably sound familiar to you. If you have worked or have been educated in the last ten to thirty years, you will see the pattern of rewarding this type of thinking in our organizations and educational institutions.

The right hemisphere, which controls the left side of the body, is simultaneous, specializes in context, and synthesizes the big picture. Without a doubt, the ability to think quickly in today's fast-paced world requires right hemisphere functions. Just as I stated in Lesson 3: Intuition, I am not advocating tossing aside the value of the left brain—our entire brain is a gift from God. I am simply seeking to focus on developing our right-brain functions. At this point, most of us have a well-developed left hemisphere. After all, we have spent most of our lifetime educated and trained to use our left brain. What we now need as leaders is to develop and reconnect with the processes of our right brain.

Dr. Edward de Bono is best known for taking the mystical subject of creativity and describing it with hard science.[26] In his book *How to Have Creative Ideas*, he discusses developing idea creativity, which is part of what he describes as *lateral thinking*:

> With logic you start out with certain ingredients just as in playing chess, you start out with given pieces. But what are those pieces? In most real life situations the pieces are not given, we just assume they are there. We assume certain perceptions, certain concepts, and certain boundaries. Lateral thinking is concerned not with playing with the existing pieces but with seeking to change those very pieces. Lateral thinking is concerned with the perception part of thinking. This is where we organize the external world into the pieces we can then "process."

Lateral thinking is perception thinking, looking for creative and innovative ways of viewing the world. This process is not constricted by boundaries and limited beliefs; it challenges us to move into expansiveness, unlimited possibilities, and abundance thinking. This is exactly the world of God—unlimited.

Moving into the world of unlimited possibilities may be uncomfortable for some of us. Our comfort zone is finite and concrete, not infinite and conceptual. The process and the functions of logical thinking look for conclusions and certainty, whereas creative thinking is visionary, looking for possibilities. In this era of leadership, why would we put constraints on our possibilities?

Right-brain, lateral thinking propels and guides self-directed learning. We will discuss the importance of personal development and growth in Lesson 15: Growth in more detail. For now, understand that innovative thinking and creating knowledge accelerates with development of the right brain.

One of the greatest benefits of right-brain development is the ability to problem solve at a higher level. Training yourself and being open to possibilities will help to shift perception at a greater speed. Activities discussed in Lesson 7: Perception Shifting and Lesson 3: Intuition will help you develop this skill. In addition to the development exercises, staying connected to your Source is the greatest way to connect to your creative energy. Problem solving and decision making at a rapid pace is part of our fabric in today's organizations.

> The process and the functions of logical thinking look for conclusions and certainty, whereas creative thinking is visionary, looking for possibilities.

Shared information often requires instant decisions at lightning speed. We can have confidence in our ability to problem solve quickly with well-developed right brains.

Practicing creativity not only helps leaders make confident decisions quickly, innovate, and problem solve; creativity also helps us interact with others at a higher level. Because creativity is a gift from God, planted in all of us, the ability to connect energetically through creativity goes immediately to our souls. When we experience someone else's creativity such as in music, film, books, or art, we feel something deep down inside. That feeling is our energy of oneness, of our connection.

> **Practicing creativity not only helps leaders make confident decisions quickly, innovate, and problem solve; creativity also helps us interact with others at a higher level.**

While earning my undergraduate degree, I took an art appreciation course. During our study of abstract art, the professor had us describe how we felt while looking at each art piece. During the exercise, if any of us would say something obvious like, "That looks like a ship," she would mark points off our grade. This was an extremely valuable lesson to learn; she challenged us to use our other senses beyond our eyes and stay in the creative side of our brain. Our logical side wanted to analyze the picture instead of conceptualizing the possibilities. I now do this practice anytime I experience art. I experience the beauty of an opera sung in another language through many senses beyond auditory. The creative energy moves from the actors to my soul, with complete understanding and clarity when I remember the lesson learned in that art appreciation course.

Living in this creative zone is as beneficial for leaders as it is for artists. Observe artists at work, whether it is performing artists, painters, sculptors, writers, or designers. Artists are present in the moment of creating with razor-sharp focus as the divine download fills the spaces of their minds, hearts, and bodies.

God gave us creativity, and through our creation, we share those gifts with others. Not only reserved for and harnessed by what you may typically think of as traditional artists, this creative zone resides in all of us. Think of the story about the creation of Post-it Notes®. Spencer Silver invented the adhesive but initially thought it was not strong enough. Later, Silver's colleague, Arthur Fry, needed a bookmark for his church hymnal that would not fall out. He remembered Silver's weaker adhesive and thought it would work because it was sticky enough to stay put but did not damage the hymnal pages when pulled off. Well, the rest is history, as Post-it Notes® are one of the most popular and indispensable office products of our time. Just because the invention was not immediately useful did not mean it didn't have other possible functions. The inventors remained open to infinite possibilities.

We are creative when we look for ways to motivate our teams beyond what our budgets will allow. We are creative when we work through conflict and come out better on the other side, and we are creative when we negotiate win-win outcomes.

I call on this same creative energy when I enter a meeting or I speak to an audience. Tapping into the creative flow releases energy that penetrates other people's hearts and souls. We connect through the oneness of God. Movement toward our creativity moves us closer to God.

Anytime we start to move in this direction, ego wants to interfere. Since the primary purpose of ego is to *separate*, it can work overtime as we move closer to our divinity. Ego tries to block us from creativity with negative voices such as:

- I'm not creative
- I'm too old to__(paint, dance, sculpt . . .)
- I'll wait until I__(retire, go on vacation . . .) to be creative

- I wish I had time to be creative

- Creativity is just for artists; I'm a businessperson

Ego is tricky and can rationalize us out of nearly any-thing—if we are unaware! Know this—when you tap into your God-given creativity and live in that space, you will feel great joy and satisfaction. Creativity, like God, is a mystical experience. Like deep meditation, immer-sion into your creative space may be euphoric.

> Just like deep meditation, immersion into your creative space may be euphoric.

Verve is another descrip-tion of creativity manifested outward. This creative energy expressed through artistry is a demonstration of living an inspired creative life. Verve is contagious, sparking vitality and vigorous spirit in others. Living out God's will and tapping into our Source brings all the forces of inspiration and creativity to the surface. The way we connect with people, inspiring and leading them from this state of divinity, will only add to our effectiveness as a leader. Verve is authentic, open, present, and childlike with wonder— wonder of a soul-filled, God-inspired (in spirit) life.

Practice
Play

Pablo Picasso reminds us, "Every child is an artist. The problem is how to remain an artist once he grows up." The best way to start is to do what we did as children—play. I had so much fun picking out crayons and a coloring book as an adult, although I purchased under the pretense of buying it for my niece. Let's get the creative juices flowing with the abandonment of child-like play. Your play may include painting, drawing, Play-Doh, dancing, dress-up, or whatever makes you smile.

Explore

I had a friend, Cecil, a retired army lieutenant colonel who was an imposing figure at over six feet tall. He was a rough-and-tumble looking character on the outside, but boy, did he know how to play. He played with whatever brought him joy. He made beautiful jewelry and beamed at the site of a gorgeous stone. He created the most splendid needlepoint artwork. Cecil was verve personified, and his joy and enthusiasm for creating was contagious. He found his connection to his creativity. With his creativity augmenting his left-brain skills, Cecil had a brilliant career—twice—one in the army and later as a corporate executive after his military career. His effectiveness as a leader was due in large part to his creativity.

Journal

Journaling is another way to tap into your creative energy. We have been using journaling for quiet reflection quite a bit in this course. However, journaling is a great tool to create. Get different colored pens and let the juices flow—draw, design, and write whatever comes to you.

▶ Make sure to not censor or judge what you are creating; simply enjoy the flow.

▶ Here are a few questions to reflect upon and journal about (by the way, go ahead and use the colored pens):

▶ Do you consider yourself a natural right- or left-brain thinker? How do you use your right-brain functions?

▶ How can you leverage more creativity at work? Home? Play?

▶ When was the last time you did something creative? How did it feel?

▶ What have you been dying to do? What is stopping you?

▶ What form of art touches your soul? When was the last time you had that experience? When is the next time you plan to be in that space again?

Possibility Brainstorming

Find an object, such as a paper clip, and brainstorm without judgment or censorship how many different uses you can think of for that object. I have done this many times with teams in order to shift into right-brain mode. Believe me, there are hundreds of uses for a paper clip!

Pause

You are now invited to pray, reflect, or meditate on . . .

Dear God,

Thank you for my

creativity and imagination.

Remind me through the Holy Spirit

to be childlike with wonder,

and childlike with play.

I, too, will paint this world with the

brilliance of an artist

and a heart filled with love.

Amen.

13
LESSON

ORDER

Order and simplification are the first steps towards mastery of a subject.
—Thomas Mann

Life truly begins after you have put your house in order.
—Marie Kondo

Teachings, Thoughts, and Theories

Order makes sense of chaos, and because we yearn for meaning in nearly everything we do, leaders must have order. Order does not mean confinement, rigid boundaries, and unrealistic parameters; it truly means exactly the opposite. Order helps you create realistic parameters and boundaries to help you live a joy-filled, satisfying, meaningful life. Go ahead and breathe, all my free-spirited friends—order gives us freedom!

One of my most favorite activities that I enjoy doing with clients is the *life wheel*. A sample life wheel is located in the complimentary Action Guide at *www.ACourseInLeadership.com*. Draw a circle, and evenly divide the circle into eight sections. Label each of the eight sections with one of the following categories: **Order gives us freedom.** *health*, *home*, *career*, *recreation*, *relationships*, *money*, *service*, and *spirituality*. The whole circle with these eight categories represents your full life.

Now draw another circle and use these same categories, but this time divide the circle to reflect how you spend your time in these areas. This second circle represents your life today, at this moment. Is it still in balance? Is your career taking up most of the circle and leaving barely enough room to write in the other seven categories? Where would you like to make changes to bring your full life into balance and order? What chaos is inhibiting your freedom?

I know there is quite a bit of talk going around about *balance*. Unfortunately, the discussion only seems to pile on guilt because many of us are already aware that we are out of balance. The purpose of this lesson is not to engender guilt, but to help a miracle come into your life with awareness and practical strategies to regain order and balance.

Let's look to nature for our lesson in balance. Nature teaches us about seasons. Our life also has seasons. Many times our seasons are busy, other times our seasons may offer renewal, and sometimes our seasons may call for hibernation. Seasons do not go on forever—there is *always* a change of season. Listen and learn this lesson from nature: you cannot continue indefinitely at a frenetic pace sheerly by adrenaline; it is unnatural and could be extremely dangerous.

Nature also teaches us that unless we shed the old way, we cannot begin anew. This is nature's miracle—shifting. A caterpillar shifts to a butterfly, and the snake sheds its skin. We cannot move forward and look for something new if we don't let go of the old; and we cannot experience the miracle of a different perspective or idea if we hold on to old and limiting beliefs.

Nature also teaches us that unless we shed the old way, we cannot begin anew.

We spend a lot of time in leadership and management seminars discussing how to prioritize. Many of us have handled this lesson fairly well at work, but we forget the idea of adding balance to this equation. Like the balance of seasons, we can work at a fast pace for a while, meeting deadlines and seizing opportunities. Without seeing the bigger picture, however, we could end up spinning our wheels on the *perceived* priority, and everything else goes to pot. That is where order comes into play. Without order, we will continue to overlook commitments, even with our priority list.

We gain order in our spaces by decluttering. When we have too much clutter, we block creativity, insight, and energy flow. We have excessively too much paper clutter, including email and virtual paper. Paper piles up in our offices, homes, cars, handbags, briefcases, and wallets without orderly approaches to eliminate or avoid this drain. Not only do we experience an interruption to flow, but our lack of order and the clutter de-energizes us.

I love the TRASH system used by professional organizers to declutter paper:

Toss it – get rid of it

Refer it – delegate it to the appropriate person

Act on it – take care of it (moving it to another stack is *not* taking care of it)

Store it – file it in a place where you can retrieve it

Halt it – get off the mailing list (including traditional and email lists)

I like this system for its simplicity and ease. Also, recognize that procrastination could be one of the biggest ways to sabotage your success with this process. Feeling overwhelmed is a huge contributor to procrastination. If you find yourself feeling overwhelmed, stop, reflect on why, and look for support if you need it. That support could come in the form of a virtual assistant and asking friends or family members for help.

Asking for assistance is not only smart for you to do, but you also then afford someone else an opportunity to serve others—a win-win scenario for all. Another helpful strategy is chunking or breaking a large task into small, doable pieces or *chunks*. When you set these mini deadlines and complete the tasks, always remember to celebrate before you move on to the next.

In addition to finding order with your paper, create order in the spaces of your office, home, car, and any other space in which you find yourself. Again, when you clear the clutter in your physical spaces, you will find that clarity, energy, and creativity flow to you, unobstructed.

Gail Blanke gives four rules of disengagement from *things* in her book *Throw Out Fifty Things*.[27] The first rule is to determine how you feel about the items in your space. If anything hinders movement or gets in the way, or it makes you feel bad or weighs you down, then get rid of it. The second rule is addition. Ask yourself if the items add anything to your life, or are they just sitting there collecting dust? If they have no benefit, get rid of them. The KISS principle, *Keep It Super Simple*, is the third rule. When you are deciding whether to keep something or get rid of it, don't make the decision complicated. Finally, kick fear to the curb, reclaiming your order, creativity, and productivity.

As you gain order in your spaces by decluttering, sort the items by determining if you are going to keep, donate, sell, toss, or move items to their proper location. Examine each space with fresh eyes as you go from room to room and ask yourself the following questions:

- Does this artwork, furniture, or collection of accessories represent what I want to accomplish in this room, such as to relax, energize, pamper, or entertain?
- Do these clothes represent the way I want to present myself?
- How do I feel in this space? Why?

Another favorite practice for gaining order is from Marie Kondo's *The Life-Changing Magic of Tidying Up* where she discusses moving items along that are no longer needed by giving gratitude first.[28] I love her approach and have "KonMaried" many rooms in my home.

Reclaim order with your time, remembering we have 86,400 seconds each day—spend them wisely in ways that serve you. So many time management books, seminars, and classes approach time management from the framework of a new calendar, planning book, or software to "give you more time." Never in the history of our planet have we had any more or any less than twenty-four hours in a day. Time management is really about self-management (order), and self-management is about living a life of joy and satisfaction.

Making order of our calendars and our time requires us to recognize the time takers in our lives such as interruptions, *have-tos*, unrealistic expectations, other people's chaos, clutter, and not enough self-care. Develop some strategies to minimize or eliminate interruptions such as checking email only at certain times during the day, stepping away from surfing the internet or social media by reserving these activities for certain times of the day, and closing your office door

> Time management is really about self-management (order), and self-management is about living a life of joy and satisfaction.

to work—*really*! Structuring meetings with agendas and times attached to each agenda item, having only essential people attend, and pre-meeting preparation will help establish order. While establishing order with your calendar and time, I like to remember to make time my FRIEND:

Find the *why* in the task

Record everything on a list that needs accomplished

Identify your priorities

Estimate the real time necessary to complete the task and add 20%

Nail it down on the calendar

Do it!

Setting order in your life also requires balance of mind, body, and spirit. In the next lesson, we dive into these three aspects of our lives in greater depth.

Getting relationships in order is another important aspect of living and leading in balance. Start by examining the relationships in your circle, including coworkers, family, and friends. Do these people lift you up or bring you down? Are they loving and supportive, or do they drain you? Surround yourself with people who love and care about you. Author and speaker Jim Rohn said, "We are the average of the five people we spend the most time with." Choose well.

Are your finances in order? Balancing your checkbook monthly, paying your bills on time, putting money into savings, and long-term financial planning are all activities of having your finances in order. Living within your means, knowing where and how you spend money, and having a financial plan demonstrates financial responsibility at work and at home. Denial and avoidance are ego's attempt at disrupting financial order. Checking our attitude and perception about money is an important step in reclaiming and establishing financial order.

What is your relationship with money? Do you have order in your life in this area? We get so hung up on money, but money is really just an object. Why do we make money more important than it needs to be? I am not saying that we don't need money; I know we need it to pay our bills and put food into the mouths of our families. However, we have given it too much importance, allowing money's energy to put us out of balance by giving it entirely too much weight.

Think about how we give away our power when we place unnecessary importance on money. We let money keep us up at night, worrying about it. We work ourselves into early graves to keep what we have and try to get more. We have disputes, arguments, and even wars over money. We get addicted to spending and to shopping. We lie about money when the bill collectors call. We avoid paying our bills and then think about them incessantly. We criticize and judge those who have money, and then we turn around to criticize and judge those who don't have money. In all these situations, we have made *money* the central focus. What if we didn't give money that kind of attention? What if we didn't work for the money but for another reason altogether? What if we worked at something that gave us joy? What if we shifted our perspective from sales to service? What if we had a miracle in our lives to heal our fear about money?

We can.

If we accept money as just another *thing* or energy, we give it no special importance than simply another vehicle that enables us to serve. We serve others by allowing money to flow to and through us. We serve the employees of the electric company when we pay our bill. We help the families of the department store employees when we buy clothes. We help to educate our community when we pay our mortgage taxes. When we shift our *getting* or scarcity mental models to service and abundant flow, we experience miraculous healing in our relationship with money.

A common but false perception is that God wants us to be poor. Money is not the root of all evil, as people often misquote the Bible to say. Rather, "the love of money is the root of all evil," which speaks to greed. This imbalance is a division made by the ego to give money (or lack of it) too much importance. This is the ego at work. If we would shift from the scarcity mentality that money is a limited resource—one that only the rich have—

to one that recognizes God wants us to have whatever we need to live in His will, then we would find peace in our relationship with money. Order in this area comes from truth and integrity. We pay our bills on time; we tell the collection agency that we can only afford $10 a month (and then we pay it); we do not spend beyond what we truly need; and we generously help others. All these are ways to establish order with money.

Practice

Order comes into our lives by uncluttering and organizing our physical spaces to clear away the excess. We also establish order with our calendar, and money. Following are eight exercises in decluttering and establishing order in our lives:

> ▶ When you bring in the mail, sort it near a trash can, and throw away all unwanted paper, including envelopes, right away.

> ▶ File and pay your bills once a week.

> ▶ Only keep hard copies of statements and bills you cannot obtain electronically.

> ▶ Back up your computer daily or weekly.

> ▶ Go through your space room by room, drawer by drawer, with fresh eyes using Blanke's four rules of disengagement.

> ▶ Balance your checkbook and reconcile all accounts monthly. Know where your money goes. Avoid avoidance.

> ▶ Cut out excess spending, and eliminate debt. When you eliminate worrying about money, you eliminate debt.

> ▶ Create a budget and spending plan. Work with a coach or an accountability partner to keep you on track.

Pause

You are now invited to pray, reflect, or meditate on . . .

Dear God,

Into your hands

I place all worry and roadblocks

to an orderly life.

My fears about time,

letting go of stuff,

and money

are dissolved by your love.

I know by eliminating these blocks

to abundance,

my life may be

filled anew.

May I receive your

glorious gifts with

an open heart,

free of clutter,

worry,

guilt,

and fear.

I thank you.

Amen

14
LESSON

HEALTH

The greatest wealth is health.

—Virgil

*The power of love to change bodies is legendary,
built into folklore, common sense, and everyday
experience. Love moves the flesh, it pushes
matter around . . . Throughout history, "tender
loving care" has uniformly been recognized as
a valuable element in healing.*

—Larry Dossey

Teachings, Thoughts, and Theories

Health is undervalued. We take the sensation of feeling good for granted, and that *good enough* feeling propels us to keep going beyond reason like the Energizer bunny. Catholic Church Official A. J. Reb Materi wisely observed, "So many people spend their health gaining wealth, and then have to spend their wealth to regain their health." Looking at health holistically, we must understand the importance of maintaining or reclaiming health in mind, body, and spirit.

Living a healthy lifestyle is one of self-care. I am not talking about bubble baths and pedicures—although both are great fun. I am talking about loving yourself first before you take care of others. This is especially challenging for many of my female clients, because we are nurturers and helpers by nature. However, helping and nurturing require that you have a source from which to extend. If you are empty, how can you give or help?

I love to think of the airplane analogy based on when the flight attendants give us preflight directions on how to use the oxygen masks if cabin pressure drops. They don't say, "Help everyone around you first, and if there is any air left over, breathe some yourself." Of course not. They tell us to put the mask on ourselves first, and only after we stabilize, then help those around us. This is a good lesson for our mental, physical, emotional, and spiritual health and well-being.

Next to our hearts, our minds are the most powerful force in our bodies. We discussed this concept of mindfulness in Lesson 2. Our minds are powerful. Knowing this and being conscious of what we allow or put into our mind is crucial for self-care and a healthy mind. Think about a movie, show, or book you read or saw just before you went to sleep. Do you remember how you dreamt and thought about it all night? Was the content (information or images) healthy and positive, or were the thoughts destructive to your psyche? In our culture, we experience desensitization to violent images, hate-filled messages, and stress-induced content. To have a healthy mind, we must not underestimate the importance of being aware and conscious about what we invite into our minds.

> To have a healthy mind, we must not underestimate the importance of being aware and conscious about what we invite into our minds.

Two nights ago, after a beautiful meditation, I had an extremely disturbing dream. I was confused and afraid and wasn't sure what to do. I decided to pray and ask God if the dream was important information or insight He was giving me. Immediately, I felt warm and comforted in my prayer as God responded, "If you feel fearful with these thoughts, they are not of Me." In those few moments of prayer and listening, I felt a profound sense of peace and knowing. Sometimes the closer we get to our Source, the more ego will pull out the big guns. Remember, anything that comes with fear is EGO (Edging God Out).

When those fear-filled, egoic thoughts enter our minds, we can stop, meditate, and reconnect with God. Then, and only then, will we experience peace of mind and clarity. In addition to fearful thoughts, underlying beliefs that no longer serve us also contribute to an unhealthy mind.

One of the most effective ways to clear our mind of negative beliefs and thought patterns is through visualization. Recently, I was ready to release a belief that had held me back, and I used a visualization that was extremely powerful. *I was on a racetrack and saw my belief in the form of a baton. God was also on the track, manifested as a beautiful man with long, flowing hair. As the race began, I carried the belief (baton) and handed it off to God, like a relay race. He carried it as He ran, but after only a few moments, the belief dissolved in His capable hand.* This image still brings tears to my eyes as I say His love dissolved my fear-filled beliefs.

As discussed in Lesson 3: Intuition, we must develop the right hemisphere of our brain in order to have more balance in our thinking. When we develop our right brains, we will tap into creative and intuitive thoughts, both of which are essential for effective leaders. Growth and development, too, are important elements of a healthy mind. In Lesson 15: Growth, we explore the implications of personal and professional development.

Taking stock of your physical health is important so you have the stamina to lead your organization and life to your greatest potential. Key factors for your physiological health include a body weight at an ideal level for optimum health, nutritious eating, hydration, sleep, and exercise. We are probably quite well educated on proper nutrition and weight loss since we spend over $60 billion a year in the diet industry. Remember to put better food into your body than you put fuel into your car. If you still struggle with weight issues, you may have some under-lying beliefs that block you from achieving the success you may desire in this area.

Many of us walk around each day without proper hydration. We should drink at least sixty-four ounces of water a day in order for our bodies to function at an optimal level. If you live in a dry climate and you exercise, you will likely need even more water. The benefits of hydrating our bodies include efficient metabolic processes; healthy function of the heart, kidneys, and digestive systems; better regulation of body temperature; and improved transport of nutrients throughout our body. When we are de-hydrated, fatigue sets in and we feel sluggish. By making a conscious commitment to stay hydrated, you will find increased physical energy and stamina.

Restful sleep is another healthy habit, and we get too little of it. According to an article in *Success* magazine by Daniel Amen, MD, "Sleep deprivation has been associated with events such as the Exxon Valdez oil spill, the Chernobyl nuclear disaster, the British Petroleum oil spill, the Union Carbide gas leak, and even the Challenger space shuttle crash. More than 100,000 traffic accidents a year are attributed to sleep-deprivation."[29] The appropriate amount of sleep varies per individual; however, most experts recommend seven to ten hours of sleep per night. A good rule of thumb to follow is to go to bed within the same day that you got up. If you are not in the habit of getting the proper amount of sleep, some behavior modification may be necessary, but with commitment and practice, you will get there. Try some relaxation exercises prior to going to bed, as these will help you establish a new routine of quieting your mind and your body.

A good rule of thumb to follow is to go to bed within the same day that you got up.

Exercise is vitally important to your health. Our bodies are meant to move. Weight maintenance is an obvious benefit of exercise, but so is an effective and efficient cardiovascular system. Moreover, when it comes to stress management, exercise tops the list of techniques to deal with tension. Researchers have determined that the hormone cortisol, also known as the *stress hormone*, releases throughout our bodies when we experience stress. The fight-or-flight response release of cortisol also contributes to weight gain. In order to combat the release of cortisol, we release the *happy hormone*, called endorphins, during exercise.

Exercise is also great for our mental and emotional state, contributing to feelings of wellness and vitality. Remember to include stretching in your daily exercise routine to keep the muscles limber and elongated. My friend Cheryl, a massage therapist, says, "Motion is lotion for your joints." Adding weight training a couple of times per week also keeps our bones strong. Once you establish a regular habit of daily exercise, you will come to think of exercise as a part of your routine, the same as brushing your teeth.

Developing emotional health involves living in truth—truth to yourself and others. Refusing to allow other people's non-truths into your space is healthy emotional self-care. Saying *no* to invitations when you are not interested or don't have the desire or time to go are positive practices in emotional self-care.

Cultivating positive relationships contributes to emotional health and wellness. Spending time with people who love and respect you honors the magnificent person you are. Learn to recognize those relationships that drain your emotional energy. People who gossip and see themselves as victims are not taking responsibility for their choices, and they draw negative energy to themselves. Complaining and shaming are also negative emotional drainers. Again, we see these types of behaviors accompanied by negative attraction. If you don't want to attract this type of negative energy in your relationships, then expand your circle to include people with the type of energy you want surrounding you. Look for affirmative emotional energy in people who are positive energetic forces and who exhibit traits like being honest, accountable, proactive, and grateful. These emotional energetic forces will feed your emotional health in tremendous ways, propelling you to even greater leadership abilities.

Spiritual health completes our holistic approach to health and wellness. What is your relationship to your Source? From where do you get your energy, inspiration, and hope? Your responses to these questions will shift you toward examining your spiritual health. What makes you feel complete inside, nurturing your soul? What makes your heart sing or your soul stir?

Feeling a soul or spiritual connection or *in-spirit-ation* does not always mean prayer or meditation. You may be moved by art or music. For me, I love to listen to drumming—Native American, Irish, African, or Kudo drumming. My heart literally leaps when I hear drumming, touching something deep within my soul.

Sitting in stillness, whether in meditation, quiet reflection, or journaling, helps me hear that still small voice inside, the voice of unconditional love—the voice of the Holy Spirit. When I consciously nurture this practice of spiritual health, I find more connection to God throughout the day. I commit to my work with greater purpose and intent. I also have incredibly sharp focus when I am healthy in spirit. Honoring mind, body, emotions, and soul with love, self-care, and self-respect is the best spiritual practice anyone could participate in.

Remember, *you* are your best asset. If not you, then who? You are the MVP, the most valuable person you have. Step into your greatness with love and care for yourself.

Practice
Inner Wisdom

Know that your deep inner wisdom wants you to live in full health. Listen to the still small voice for guidance, strength, and purpose to make healthy choices for your mind, body, heart, and spirit. Practice quieting your mind for reflection, prayer, meditation, or stillness to recharge or refuel. Hiking, walking, or swimming are also ways to quiet the mind. Surrender your need to *do, do, do* and *go, go, go*. Remember to rest your mind and body each day. Choose foods that nourish and energize you. Keep your body strong with exercise and hydration.

Check-ups

Schedule annual visits with your doctor and dentist, and keep them. Regular checkups honor your body by examining your blood pressure, gender-specific health concerns, eyes, hearing, teeth, and overall health.

Power Hour

Integrate a power hour into your day with an easy sixty-minute program of self-care. First, spend twenty minutes feeding your mind by reading something inspirational or motivational. Then spend the next twenty minutes honoring your body with exercise and stretching. In the last twenty minutes of this hour, spend time nurturing your spirit with prayer, meditation, stillness, or whatever activity connects you with your Source. Create within your space a sacred place where you can spend this time cultivating a spiritual practice that fulfills and sustains you.

Pause

You are now invited to pray, reflect, or meditate on . . .

Dear God,

You created me in your splendor and likeness.

Help me to never forget

from where I came;

To honor my body

with physical healthy practices;

To honor my mind

with positive healthy practices;

To honor my emotional health

with insight and awareness;

and to honor my connection

to you with spiritual health.

I surrender any resistance to

healing these areas in my life.

I am open to tender loving care.

I am open to the healing light

that is yours

now and forever.

Amen.

15
LESSON
GROWTH

Intellectual growth should commence
at birth and cease only at death.
—Albert Einstein

You've got to do your own growing,
no matter how tall your grandfather was.
—Irish Saying

Teachings, Thoughts, and Theories

As a leadership coach, I am always excited when a powerful question or statement crosses my path or, better yet, when it knocks me off my feet. I remember several years ago how Seth Godin got my attention in his book *Tribes*, when he stated, "If you're not uncomfortable in your work as a leader, it's almost certain you're not reaching your potential as a leader."[30] That statement resonated with me in 2008 and still does today. He was talking about the discomfort we sometimes feel as leaders. Furthermore, when we identify the discomfort, we've found a place where we need leadership. Godin's list of uncomfortable situations includes:

- Standing up in front of strangers
- Proposing an idea that may fail
- Challenging the status quo
- Resisting the urge to settle

I do love those moments that move me out of my comfort zone and into what I call a *seat-stirring* state. I know when I start stirring or squirming, I am onto something, and that something is usually growth.

Of course, I also like to state things in a positive frame, so my list may look something like:

- Motivating people in the direction of a shared goal
- Creating and innovating with others, living in a synergy zone

- Thinking outside the box and trying something that "hasn't been done before"

- Pushing myself and others to live in creativity and authenticity, even when it may be more work

Why is it so important to push ourselves outside our comfort zone? Because, as Benjamin Franklin stated many years ago, "When you're finished changing, you're finished." His profound statement in our rapidly changing world is more relevant today than ever. What worked ten years ago doesn't work today. In fact, what worked last year probably doesn't work today. The challenge for us in our organizations is to stay in a constant state of learning *or* our organizations will no longer exist.

In chapter six on Openness, I described MIT professor Peter Senge's five key steps for an organization to be in a state of growth.[31] According to Senge, the necessary steps include personal mastery (continuous individual learning), mental models (identifying individual perceptions), shared vision, team learning, and systems thinking (seeing the big picture). As described in Lesson 4: Intention, Japanese professors Nonaka and Nishiguchi defined the concept of ba, which is the energy necessary for innovation and learning to take place.[32] Ba needs love, care, trust, and compassion in the environment to exist. If we are going to lead our organizations while in a learning or growth state, we must begin by *first* developing and growing ourselves. Of course, we must do this with love, care, trust, and connection.

To stretch outside of your comfort zone, you must trust that you'll be okay and love yourself enough to try. Don't get me wrong, you may fail; *but so what—you only fail.* You will be in good company:

- Abraham Lincoln failed in business twice, had a nervous breakdown, and was defeated in eight elections before he was elected the sixteenth president of the United States.

- Lucille Ball was dismissed from drama school because she was "too shy."
- The Beatles were turned down by Decca Records because the label didn't like their sound, and "guitar sound was on its way out."
- Ulysses S. Grant failed as a soldier, farmer, and real estate agent, and then worked for his father as a handyman at the age of thirty-eight.
- A teacher told Thomas Edison that he "was too stupid to learn anything."
- Walt Disney was fired from a newspaper because he "lacked imagination."
- Mark Victor Hansen and Jack Canfield were turned down by over 140 publishers for their *Chicken Soup for the Soul* book, now over $1.3 billion in sales.
- Marilyn Monroe was dropped by 20th Century Fox in her first year because she "was unattractive and couldn't act."
- Henry Ford's first two companies were failures.

Fear of failure is allowing ego to rule.

In order to stretch our growth and learning, we must step outside of our comfort zone. I remember being petrified early in my business as I met with a potential client. He was the CEO of a large international organization. I thought, *What am I doing here? I am not smart enough to be here.* These thoughts and similar ones raced through my head. We ended up having a good meeting even though I did not get the consulting contract that time. I was disappointed in myself for succumbing to the negative voices in my head. As we approach our higher self, moving ever closer to our relationship with God, ego goes into overdrive and works against us. We must remain aware and alert to these negative voices and distinguish between comfort and fear. With the awareness of negative voices and ego's attempts to keep me in my comfort zone, I've learned to break through. Each time I am on the other side of the uncomfortable situation, I feel a sense of pride and accomplishment.

Sometimes we become comfortable with the perception of *staying put*. This is what is referred to as the *boiled frog syndrome*.[33] If you put a frog into boiling water, he will immediately jump out. However, if you put a frog into room temperature water and bring the water to a slow boil, the frog becomes lethargic, complacent, and ultimately cooks. Staying put is a false perception of staying comfortable. We cannot just stay static; it is impossible in a world that is always in evolution. If we do not move forward, the only other direction is backward.

Staying put is a false perception of staying comfortable.

Conscious, strategic decisions to develop and grow personally, professionally, and spiritually will only make us better leaders in this new era. We must approach this growth plan with love, care, trust, and compassion as we undertake movement outside of our comfort zone. Join a group of like-minded individuals for shared learning and support. Attend workshops, seminars, and retreats to expand your growth and development in mind, body, and spirit. We can attend worldwide events from the comforts of our own homes or offices via the internet. In many of the online courses that I teach, students from all around the world attend class and share their experiences, creating a richer learning environment for all attendees.

Conscious, strategic decisions to develop and grow personally, professionally, and spiritually will only make us better leaders in this new era.

Failing to plan is planning to fail. Let's work on a development plan to assist in your growth professionally, personally, and spiritually.

Practice
Development Plan

When designing a development plan, whether it is for professional, personal, or spiritual growth, the steps are the same. A few key elements to remember when creating your development plan:

- Always begin with reflection.
- For goal setting, use SMART goals. The elements of SMART goals are:
  - Specific
  - Measurable
  - Aligned with values
  - Realistic
  - Time-bound (attached to dates)
- Find a coach or accountability partner to work with.
- Celebrate each successful completion of your goal.
- Be open to learn, and seize opportunities that were not planned by you.
- Remember to practice gratitude.

Now let's look at the ten steps to create your growth development plan.

Step 1: Reflection—Identify and reflect upon:
  - What is your vision of an ideal leader?
    - List those qualities, attributes, attitudes, and behaviors.

- ∘ What are the antitheses or opposites of your ideal leader?
- ▶ Whom do you admire as a leader? Why?
- ▶ Who are your role models? What about them do you admire?
- ▶ List your leadership strengths.
- ▶ Define areas you would like to develop.
- ▶ List behaviors you wish to develop.
- ▶ List behaviors that no longer serve you and that you would like to do less.
- ▶ Be aware of your emotions and energy as you reflect upon each response.

Step 2: Identify your goals and remember to use the SMART goal framework discussed above. For each of your SMART goals, apply steps 3 through 10.

Step 3: List the necessary steps you need to achieve your goal.

Step 4: List past successes or strengths to remind you that you *can* achieve the goal.

Step 5: List people or resources you have available for support.

Step 6: List strengths, support, and resources upon which you could draw if you stumble.

Step 7: List any weaknesses or blocks that could potentially cause you to stumble.

Step 8: List the value, reasons why, and benefits that fuel your desire to achieve the goal.

Step 9: Describe in detail what the end-state of achieving your goal looks and feels like.

Step 10: Celebrate!

Continued Education

Speaking as a professional, I believe that continued education is imperative for expanding the mind. This learning does not necessarily require formal degrees, although it could. Continuing education opportunities abound with many professional organizations. A day does not go by where I do not receive an invitation to a webinar, seminar, or class. Many of these educational opportunities occur virtually with a worldwide audience. I recently spoke at a virtual seminar with attendees from all around the globe. The other speakers also presented from different corners of world, all attending from the comforts of their homes and offices. Many of these virtual learning opportunities are offered at little to no cost to participants.

Professional Organizations

Seek out professional organizations that align with your values, vision, and perhaps represent where you want to be. Take advantage of their libraries; many of these resources are rich with articles about industry trends, challenges, and best practices. Several organizations have online discussion boards for support, quick focus groups, and shared information.

Networking

In addition to the vast resources of these professional organizations, networking opportunities sprout organically from these associations to include affiliate programs, partnerships, and collaboration. If you feel you cannot afford the membership fees, seek out ways that you can volunteer with the organizations of your choice. Some online networking sites, such as LinkedIn, are free to join, and once you are there, you can join a plethora of organizations via the site. Again, the information and resources shared on many web-based organizations are great opportunities for learning and development growth.

Local Level

Don't forget to get involved at your local level, too. Joining local community organizations, such as the chamber of commerce, affords you opportunities to network with and learn from other leaders and professionals. My consulting, training, and coaching company conducts mastermind groups where we strategically invite people from several different industries to be in the same room together, expanding their knowledge with best practices, problem solving, and support. The synergy and ba that come from these experiences never cease to delight and surprise me.

Share

Share your knowledge with others. Write articles, teach a workshop, or volunteer at a local school. When we teach others, our knowledge expands exponentially. We discuss more about sharing knowledge in Lesson 17: Teaching. Spend some time with retirees who've had long careers and many experiences. Learning from those who have gone before us is a form of wisdom and honor.

Try It, You May Like It

Personally, your knowledge and growth can expand in any direction you choose—you get to design the steps to your growth. In addition, you will learn even more with your surrender and openness to the wisdom of God. A few ideas for personal growth:

- ▶ Join book-discussion clubs or create your own.
- ▶ Attend special-interest classes at your community college.

- ▶ Learn another language.
- ▶ Volunteer.
- ▶ Take up a new hobby.
- ▶ Teach a hobby.
- ▶ Travel, including local destinations.
- ▶ Join a club.
- ▶ Learn yoga or tai chi.
- ▶ Paint, draw, sculpt, or do anything else to get your hands creating.

Come on, what is it? What is it you've been dying to do? Remember the Nike advertisements, and *Just Do It!* I am sure you could easily add to this list. Do something outside of your comfort zone. Once that gets comfortable, look for ways to expand.

Spiritual Growth

To grow spiritually, take on a practice to be still, and listen. Only you know what form of practice is best for you. My dear friend Michael, a Buddhist, claims he cannot meditate in the traditional manner—sitting still in a quiet place. His meditation is hiking. He connects to his Source in deep, meaningful ways when he hikes. In the same way, I experience a thoughtful connection to God when I swim laps in the pool. The rhythmic sound of my hands hitting the water is calming and centering. I love that time spent in spiritual awareness.

Retreats

If you wish to train yourself to achieve a meditative awareness, attend a spiritual retreat alone. You will not be tempted to socialize with others if you attend solo. If it feels right to you, attend a spiritual retreat with others and share in the collective insight you gain. Again, find what works for you. There is no one single path to connecting with God. You must find what is authentic for you. Learn about other people's paths to spiritual growth. You may gain insight and wisdom by learning from other cultures and belief systems.

> There is no one single path to connecting with God. You must find what is authentic for you.

Be open, grateful, and surrender. Growth and insight will follow.

Pause

You are now invited to pray, reflect, or meditate on . . .

Dear God,

In your love,

I grow.

In your light,

I grow.

In your will,

I grow.

Dissolve in your hands

any fear or blocks

that keep me from you.

Amen.

16

LESSON

WISDOM

Reality is merely an illusion, albeit a very persistent one.
—**Albert Einstein**

Wise is that person who sees reality behind the illusion.
—**The Buddha**

Teachings, Thoughts, and Theories

Wisdom is circular. We receive it, put it out there, live it, and receive it again. Wisdom is not an achievement where we check the box and move on; it is not an arrival. We taste it and we know of it as we travel on the journey. Wisdom is a process, and not one that is ever truly finished. In actuality, the more we learn, the more we learn what we don't know. Socrates knew that when he said, "The only true wisdom is in knowing you know nothing." Enter—wisdom.

We may think of wisdom as knowledge plus experience. We know how to cultivate knowledge by applying many of the concepts from Lesson 15: Growth. We also know that our experiences go through the perceptual process. Wisdom brings those two aspects together and makes sense of the stimuli that we experience. While wisdom brings together two forms of external learning—knowledge and experience—it is a deeply internal process.

Surrender is freedom.
Surrender is liberation.
Surrender is peace.

Wisdom also requires us to be open and to grow, because without those elements, we cannot have experiences from which to learn. The Tao Te Ching describes this concept, "If you want to become whole, let yourself be partial. If you want to become straight, let yourself be crooked. If you want to become full, let yourself be empty." We can only experience the true meaning of partial, crooked, and empty with complete surrender and abandonment to God. Only through that door can we discover real wisdom, real power, and real choice. Surrender is freedom. Surrender is liberation. Surrender is peace.

Wisdom starts and ends within us. We find freedom from ego, from illusion within ourselves—in stillness. Wisdom is both silent and strong. We pass wisdom down from generation to generation, but until we internalize it and live it, wisdom lies dormant.

As a leadership coach, I ascribe to the belief that we all have inner wisdom. Part of my job is to help others to see theirs and to bring it forward. This is not a new concept:

- "If one is seeking wisdom, there is no need to leave home." —The Tao Te Ching

- "Wisdom comes to those who are calm and tranquil in spirit, to those who wait upon the Lord. Through an ever-increasing love in the heart, you will grow wise." —Saying of White Eagle

- "Dormant forces are awakened and you find yourself to be a better person than you ever imagined." —Patanjali

- "The foolish reject what they see, not what they think; the wise reject what they think, not what they see . . . Observe things as they are and don't pay attention to other people." —Huang-Po

- "When ignorance is overcome through knowledge of the Self, God is revealed." —The Bhagavad Gita

A wise leader knows that we are ever-changing beings and that everything around us is ever changing as well. We must remain flexible and not rigid, soft and not hard. The Tao teaches us to remain flexible and flowing so we can be receptive to new ideas and insight, the paradox of what is soft is strong.

Wisdom is humility. I am not talking about a false sense of demure or subservient behavior. Humility is the quiet knowing, the inner wisdom to continue learning from those who have gone before, from those who are currently present, and by listening to the Holy Spirit. Knowing that we do not have all the answers is humbling. Empowering others is an act of humility. One of my favorite leadership quotes from Lao Tzu addresses both humility and wisdom:

> As for the best leaders, the people do not notice their existence. The next best, the people honor and praise. The next, the people fear, and the next, the people hate. When the best leader's work is done, the people say, We did it ourselves!

Wisdom is a conscientious pursuit to gain insight and make sense of knowledge and experience. Diligence is required to reflect regularly, communing with the Holy Spirit and seeking out your inner wisdom. Wisdom does not fall on the lazy; it is only gained by seekers. Inspirational speaker and author Iyanla Vanzant once said, "All are called, few choose to listen." Be alert and ready, diligently seeking wisdom.

Wisdom is a conscientious pursuit to gain insight and make sense of knowledge and experience.

Practice
Reflection

Wisdom begins by looking in the mirror, literally and figuratively. Wisdom must begin with self-awareness and self-reflection. What do you see? What do you like? What do you love about yourself? Self-acceptance of the person you are paves the path to wisdom. Acceptance neutralizes judgment and criticism, both of which are impediments to gaining wisdom. When we look upon others through the veil of judgment and criticism, we are simply seeing reflections of ourselves, observing aspects of ourselves that we don't like or with which we are uncomfortable. Awareness of these moments, coupled with deep self-reflection, increase our wisdom about ourselves, others, leadership, and life.

Commitment

Committing to time for contemplation is vital in seeking wisdom. Not only will you be able to wrap your experiences and learning in quiet reflection, but also you can blend reflection with your inner wisdom and the still small voice within. To be in your right mind, be aware of ego, and go inward to where the Holy Spirit resides. In your place of divinity, you will find wisdom.

As you do the work with your contemplative practice, record your thoughts and insights in your journal. Do you see any patterns or beliefs emerge that give you clarity or insight? Are there patterns of behavior that block you from peace and joy? Reflect on your responses, familiarizing yourself with your physiological and emotional reactions. What can you learn from these reactions? Trust your inner wisdom to provide insight and clarity.

Wisdom Seekers

Seek out other wisdom seekers. Find those seekers of wisdom in the present and those from the past who can go to the doorway of wisdom with you. Whom do you admire for their wisdom and insight? Build a library of books written by and about those people. A good place to start is with the books of ancient philosophers, teachers, poets, saints, and luminaries. Spiritual texts are also full of insight steeped in wisdom. Add historical books to your library so you may learn from those who went before you. Read texts about different cultures to gain wisdom from various perspectives and mental models. I have a list of my favorites in the Action Guide to *A Course in Leadership:*

21 Spiritual Lessons on Power, Love, and Influence at *www. ACourseInLeadership.com.*

Does your current circle include wisdom seekers? Are they reading for insight or for entertainment? Be conscious of what you choose to fill your mind and with whom you choose to spend your time. Are you moving forward or moving backward? Remember that static is a false perception and does not exist.

> Be conscious of what you choose to fill your mind and with whom you choose to spend your time.

Be open and without judgment for insights that come to you—also known as *aha!* moments. Insight into wisdom is often not subtle; you know it when it hits you. When we are in a state of wisdom seeking, we are open and without judgment—ready, willing, and able for *aha!* moments to open our hearts and our minds.

Be aware that wisdom may come from places you may not think of, such as when observing a baby, watching a squirrel, or seeing cells divide. Socrates told us, "Wisdom begins in wonder." Be open and ready with the wonder of a child. Jesus told us that unless we are like children, we cannot enter the kingdom of heaven. In other words, unless we have the wonder, open mind, and open heart that is clear of judgment and false perceptions, we will not find our divine happiness.

We find great wisdom in serving others, as written in the Apocryphon of James, "Seek wisdom earnestly through learning. Practice wisdom by being faithful, loving, and charitable." Service to others is such an important lesson of leadership that we will explore more fully in the upcoming Lesson 18: Service.

Share It, and Share It Again

As leaders, we are called to share wisdom with others. This is one of the key elements sought after in leadership, yet I am surprised and hard-pressed to find the word wisdom included in many leadership books. I have taught MBA courses for nearly twenty years and have read dozens of leadership books and rarely if ever find the words *wisdom* or *love*. Wisdom is typically a historical and spiritual discussion.

Knowledge is taught; wisdom is learned. The wise leader understands the essential ingredient of wisdom. It is time to include wisdom in conjunction with leadership. Be open for wisdom to come into your mind and heart. Knowledge is taught; wisdom is learned.

Pause

You are now invited to pray, reflect, or meditate on . . .

Dear God,

It is through the Holy Spirit

that I seek wisdom

and understanding

of my leadership purpose.

It is through your love

that I am able to

apply wisdom

and share insight

with others.

Let me see the extraordinary

in the ordinary.

Let me always seek

my highest good

in you.

Amen.

17

LESSON

TEACHING

Who dares to teach must never cease to learn.
—John Cotton Dana

Whoever travels without a guide needs two
hundred years for a two-day journey.
—Rumi

Teachings, Thoughts, and Theories

Mature leadership involves responsible actions for your organization and those whom you lead. Caring for the future of the organization and the lives of your team is good stewardship; it is taking care of business. Teaching, coaching, and mentoring equip your team for the future and set up the organization responsibly with leaders for both today and tomorrow. Funny thing about teaching—we teach whether we are conscious of it or not. Like leadership, we teach by our behavior, actions, and by the demonstration of how we choose to live our lives.

I knew that good stewardship of a company meant to be financially responsible in how the company handled their money. However, several years ago I learned about stewardship in a new light when an amazing cave discovery of Kartchner Caverns opened to the public for viewing. Many years of buzz and mystery surrounded the incredible and pristine cave and the treasures it contained. I attended an early, private viewing of the cave because the corporation I worked for was a financial contributor.

Before this private showing, the tour guide gave us a lesson on the importance of being good stewards, preserving the cave and contents for future generations. We were given gloves to wear with a twofold purpose. First, the gloves served as a reminder not to touch anything, and second, if we accidently touched something, the oils from our hands would not damage the incredible and delicate formations of this living cave. Just like stewardship in an organization, as leaders we must preserve the organization for years to come, remembering to handle the precious interior (our people) with tender-loving care.

192 A Course in Leadership

Through stewardship, we teach accountability. Many leaders with whom I work struggle with the action of holding their teams accountable. Lack of accountability creates a culture of blame, avoidance, and poor communication. Accountability is self-responsibility, it is energizing, and it is conducive to creating and innovating. To teach accountability, you must make sure team members have the appropriate authority for what they are held accountable.

Practice setting SMART goals (discussed in Lesson 15: Growth), and get the commitment from your team to reach the goals. Plan to set checkpoints with team members to review progress. Provide helpful and specific feedback, and always remember to discuss the team's wins, as well as areas in which they may need additional support. Accountability is empowering and necessary in developing stewardship throughout the organization.

I love the Buddhist saying, "When the student is ready, the teacher will appear." In my many years of teaching formal courses at the university level, I am a student right along with the class I am teaching. When I teach, I learn. I have yet to teach a class where I have not learned something from my many teachers, also known as my students. As discussed in a previous lesson, we are ever changing in this world, and the cycle of learning and teaching never changes, unless of course we find ourselves closed off from learning. In order to be a good teacher, we must first be a good student.

In order to be a good teacher, we must first be a good student.

As we teach, we must remember that we are not transmitting information—*we are transforming lives*. That may sound a bit dramatic, but that is exactly what good teaching does; it transforms. Transformation comes about through many different forms: motivation, persuasion, mobilization, influence, and of course, miracles. When we teach, we are in essence saying, *I care about you, you are important, and I want to help.* Wow, who wouldn't be motivated with that type of message? Motivation also comes from demonstrating belief in others. Teaching affords us an opportunity to build esteem and self-efficacy. Think of Maslow's needs hierarchy; esteem and self-actualization are the highest levels. Teaching and learning meet high-order needs both for yourself and for those whom you teach.

Through the process of teaching, we build trust when we facilitate teaching with a learner-centered approach. Remembering that we are not only transferring information but transforming others; we teach according to the needs of others. I use the same approach when I do training, coaching, or motivational speaking. First, I discover the needs of the audience and tailor my work to meet those needs. Of course, I provide resources and information to support their transformation, but *first* I must find out where they are stuck and where they want to grow.

Effective teachers in a classroom setting know this principle and adjust their lesson plans to accommodate emerging needs that arise during instruction. We call these moments *teachable moments*, when we can seize the opportunity and use it as a springboard for learning. A Native American saying illustrates this concept, *Tell me and I'll forget. Show me, and I may not remember. Involve me, and I'll understand.* Once we identify the needs of the people and address those needs, then learning occurs and the outcome is performance.

One of the most effective ways to teach is through storytelling. Storytelling captivates the senses. Throughout history, the art of storytelling demonstrates this powerful technique used to teach. Aristotle, Plato, Jesus, Buddha, Lao Tzu, Rumi, Gibran, Hemingway, Emerson, Bob Dylan, and Smokey Robinson have mesmerized us with their gifted storytelling. This form of teaching enchants us through our feelings, connecting with us through our hearts. The emotional heart tug we get with good stories heightens our attention and holds us captive. We are fully present in those captive moments of a great story, giving our undivided attention to the details. This technique presents an incredible opportunity for the learner to not only be present with full attention, but also to retain the information, ready to call upon it when needed.

An ironic yet valuable benefit of storytelling is that the audience (the learner) is present in the *moment* of learning, *and* the story helps us prepare for *future* use of the content. When we learn from stories, we learn how they may relate to us. This is a critical element to successful storytelling: the ability to relate. When we teach through stories, we are essentially saying, *"When Ann experienced this event, she felt_____, and when she did_____, she was successful. So when you feel_____, try as Ann did and_____, because you too may be successful!"* This mental process the learner experiences helps them to remember the story concept because they are relating it to themselves.

Stories put information into context. The story I shared at the beginning of this lesson was about a cave and not about leadership; however, what appeared to be unrelated helped to put the concept of stewardship into perspective. Storytelling simplifies complex ideas, helping learners discover context, meaning, and applicability. Stories, metaphors, and allegories are processed in the right hemisphere of our brain, which appeals directly to our heart and emotions. This phenomenon is inspiring to learners, resulting in motivation and mobilization. We naturally want to

Storytelling highlights meaning without defining it.

move into action when we are inspired. Storytelling highlights meaning without defining it. When we teach through stories, we empower the learner to synthesize the information on their own, without telling them how they should think or feel about it.

Teaching by allowing and inviting our learners to process information in ways that are meaningful to them is not only smart practice, but also a wise one. Kahlil Gibran wrote in *The Prophet*, "If he [the teacher] is indeed wise, he does not bid you enter the house of his wisdom, but rather leads you to the threshold of your own mind."[34] This methodology aligns with the principles of coaching and mentoring. Both forms enhance learning by empowering learners to come to their own conclusions, thus increasing their self-efficacy. In coaching, teaching occurs through mirroring and supporting self-directed learning. Coaching helps others develop their own personal mastery in areas where they desire to grow by providing the space for learning, exploring, and discovery. In both mentoring and coaching, leader-provided resources help the learner to reach their goals.

Wise words from Einstein summarize the most effective strategy for teaching: "Example isn't another way to teach, it is the only way to teach." We share our life experiences with others by the way we choose to live our lives. Growing up, I often heard my mother say to me that *actions speak louder than words*. Our actions are the best teaching tool we own. The extremely important element here is to be conscious of the examples we give to others by choosing our behaviors, attitudes, and actions with wisdom and love.

Teaching is legacy. Learning is legacy in motion.

Teaching is legacy. Learning is legacy in motion.

Practice
Storytelling

As always, let's start with self-reflection. Do you tell stories? How effective are you at storytelling? What are your strengths and your areas for improvement when it comes to storytelling? When was the last time you told a story? What were the reactions of your intended audience?

Identify a story you believe to be a good one, and see if you can find the six elements of effective storytelling. Effective teaching through storytelling should include the following steps:

1. Describe the main characters. Include yourself because when leaders are humble, open, and willing to share stories portraying themselves as human and vulnerable, it helps them connect with their team.

2. Portray the situation, challenge, or problem in detail. Explain what is at stake with the issue.

3. Reveal the characters' intentions, thoughts, and feelings with the situation. Also, express what their thoughts are with potential outcomes and how they feel about what is at stake.

4. Explain the actions taken by the character, including the good, the bad, and the ugly. The more in depth you are with the description of the actions, the more you may heighten the learner's interest in the outcome.

5. Discuss the tools that the characters used to take action. Include which tools worked and which ones did not. Keep in mind that the tools may be thoughts, perspectives, strategies, and so forth.

6. Finally, share the outcome.

Remember to employ emotions such as laughter, joy, worry, or concern as you illustrate the story. Emotions connect directly to our hearts. We don't always remember someone's words, but we *always* remember how we felt. Above all else, be authentic as you teach the story.

Storytellers

Identify someone you believe to be an effective storyteller. Watch, observe, and study their techniques. If possible, ask that person to mentor you in the art of storytelling.

Write the Article

Write an article or blog post about a success story in your organization. Use the six steps above to frame your story.

Mentor

Mentor someone. Discover what they like to do, along with their strengths and areas in which they would like to grow. What are their feelings about learning? Together, determine what three steps they can do to gain esteem and self-efficacy in those areas. Create an action plan with them, including SMART goals, necessary steps and resources to achieve the goals, needed support, possible blocks, and what the end state of achieving the goal might look and feel like. Become an accountability partner to your mentee and celebrate their success.

Your Legacy

How important is it to you to leave a legacy? Describe your legacy. Don't rush through this exercise. List all the elements that make up your desired legacy. Identify what steps are necessary to complete your legacy. How can you live your legacy right now?

Commit to it, and create an action plan for your legacy, including the steps described in the above paragraph.

As you reflect on your legacy and the way you teach by your life choices, ponder these words:

- "You must be the change you wish to see in the world." —Gandhi
- "The world will change through you. No other means can save it." —*A Course in Miracles*

Pause

You are now invited to pray, reflect, or meditate on . . .

Dear God,

You are the great teacher,

the one who opens our minds

and our hearts.

Teach us to

always turn toward

love of ourselves

and love of others.

Teach us to live and lead by example and heal

the false sense of ourselves

so we may fully stand

in your light.

Teach through us

as instruments of your love and peace.

I am the change

I wish to see in the world.

Amen.

18 LESSON

SERVICE

I don't know what your destiny will be, but one thing I know: The ones among you who will be really happy are those who have sought and found how to serve.

—Albert Schweitzer

Let me pass, I have to follow them, I am their leader.

—Alexandre Ledru-Rollin

Teachings, Thoughts, and Theories

I always like to start my classes with a question: *Why would we talk about service in a course in leadership?* For so long, leadership functioned under the old models of leadership—when leaders were the ones being served. Wise leaders know the opposite is true.

Organizational and leadership models throughout history, and still today, are like authoritarian kingdoms. The ruling king or queen sits on their throne (corner office in the executive suite), and the serfs and subjects (subordinates and "team") support them in any way necessary. Oh, we have the right words today—*team*, *collaboration*, and *empowerment*. Unfortunately, in many organizations, actions do not match the words. We know consciously and unconsciously these models do not work; however, we do not know how to replace them. As always, we simply must turn away from fear and stare right into the face of love. In those beautiful eyes of love, we find our answers.

Service paves the path of leadership. Through love and a love-based leadership model, we serve others, our source, and ourselves. To make this miraculous shift in our perception about service, we must consciously be aware of leading with a service mindset versus a sales mindset. Many leaders I know lead with a sales mentality, seeking "buy-in" from those they lead. They obtain buy-in through persuasion, manipulation, and control. These techniques can be effective, but the leader will not get long-term commitment. A service mentality shifts from *What can you do for me?* to *What can I do for you?* This is like the phenomenon in marketing and product development happening today. *Find out what they want and we'll build it* replaces the old mental model of *build it and they will come.* Leadership focus is on service, instead of self-interest. Uh-oh . . . the ego is not going to like this! Exactly.

When leaders shift from sales to service mindsets, organizations shift from a kingdom culture and hierarchical structure to *community.* I am not describing utopia or something found only through rose-colored glasses; I am describing what can be and what *is* in some organizations and communities. By serving and giving, we are more successful. The more we give, the more we receive; the more we serve, the more we are served. This again demonstrates that whatever you put your attention toward, you will manifest.

> When leaders shift from sales to service mindsets, organizations shift from a kingdom culture and hierarchical structure to *community.*

A few years ago, a wildfire raced through the canyon where we live. What I remember most was how deeply immersed the community (individuals and organizations) was in service to one another through love. Thousands were evacuated, and homes and businesses were lost. It was the largest fire in the country at the time. Firefighters from all over the United States came to assist. The fire raged for more than a week. More powerful than the smoke that filled the air was the love, compassion, and service that enveloped the community. Everyone had a home to stay in and food to eat—even the horses and pets had a place to stay. The more we gave to each other, the more we received. Food, clothes, supplies, and money poured in. Supplies were so plentiful that a warehouse the size of a large box store was set up at a local window-and-door manufacturing site. Both the evacuees and the firefighters would go to the warehouse to *shop* (of course, no money was exchanged) for whatever they needed. Often overcome with emotions at the resources and smiling faces who warmly greeted them, firefighters from all around the country consistently commented on how they had never seen a community pull together at this level before. The more we gave, the more we received.

With a focus on service, leaders invite others to co-create and co-design organizations and communities. We do this through empowerment. Let's explore what empowerment really means. Empowerment is to give or share power. I know this concept sometimes makes leaders nervous. Power is, well, powerful. Just like attention, intention, and attraction—the more we give it away, the more we receive.

It is important to remember that as we share power, we also share responsibility. Full empowerment comes with full responsibility. We share both the delivery outcomes and the responsibility for our customers to have quality experiences. We share the creation of our goods and services, and we share the creation of our corporate or community culture. We are not subjects or serfs in empowered organizations; we are a community.

Power is a hot topic. Not all power is equal. Bertram Raven and John French identified five different power bases: legitimate, coercive, expert, reward, and referent.[35] Legitimate power is the type of power that comes with a title or position. Coercive power is one that imposes force on others, like the king who threatens to behead those who disobey. Expert power is the type of power that comes with knowledge or information that someone else does not have. Reward power comes from bestowing upon someone something of value, and referent power is the power of respect. Like anything else in this world, all forms of power can be for the greater good or for selfish and egoic purpose.

> Full empowerment comes with full responsibility.

While *empowerment* may make some leaders nervous, it also makes some followers uncomfortable. In *Scenes from Corporate Life*, Earl Shorris wrote, "Men who cannot conceive a happiness of their own accept a definition imposed upon them by others."[36] We have been taught for too long to let others define our thoughts, feelings, jobs, lives, and meaning for us. What to think, what to wear, how to feel—is it any wonder we get nervous when we receive permission or power to design these aspects for ourselves? As leaders, we must teach. We teach and show others how to stand in this power. We invite them in to learn, to grow, to create, and to commit to a purpose greater than our own. When we create and commit to the larger purpose, we seek the greater good. We become a community of *we* and *our* instead of *me* and *mine*.

In addition to co-creating culture and communities, shared delivery of outcomes, and quality customer experiences, leaders must distribute rewards. Compensation based on outcomes is a natural extension of empowerment. With this shift in power and compensation models, we need to make sure communication is strong to serve our teams so they reach their fullest potential. Flatter organizational structures, transparency, and full disclosure are necessary for organizations to shift toward a service mindset and model. Leaders become coaches, resource providers, and support for the greater good. Leaders move from a patriarchal role to a partnership role. Service thinking requires a new social contract. We no longer tell others what is meaningful; we help them discover and find the meaning for themselves. The result? Organizations and communities have whole selves who show up. And *we* show up, fully engaged, full of meaning and hope—it is a good day. We are ready.

Do not confuse the idea of service with poverty. Ego would have us believe that God demands that everyone must divest himself or herself of every material thing and that we can only experience heaven if we are poor. This message has been greatly misunderstood. When we love money more than we love God, we experience hell. That is why many wealthy people say they still don't have happiness. This has nothing to do with money, as money is simply an object. It has everything to do with where we place our focus, attention, and *love*. When we serve, we are served. When we give, we receive, just as the Chinese proverb states, "A bit of fragrance always clings to the hand that gives you roses."

Have you noticed the growing emphasis on social responsibility in our business culture?

Consumers, employees, and leaders are demanding socially responsible behavior of themselves and others. If companies choose not to comply with our wishes, we go elsewhere—because we can. We see social responsibility manifested in the philanthropic activities organizations are doing; and they are not just writing checks to nonprofits. Companies are building schools, putting shoes on children, and teaching third-world countries how to harvest water. We have business models emerging with the primary purpose of serving others. Guess what? These businesses are making money! They have learned how to connect the heart with the bank account.

> Social responsibility is not just a fad or a trend; it is an awakening, a collective consciousness showing up and stepping forward.

We also see the socially responsible movement in organizations manifested as the green movement. Entire global organizations are working their strategic plans to reduce their carbon footprint. Organizations are working with suppliers and manufacturers who share the same service and stewardship values. Social responsibility is not just a fad or a trend; it is an awakening, a collective consciousness showing up and stepping forward. This collective voice is saying *ENOUGH! If not now, when?* It is time.

In service, we listen. In service, we open. In service, we teach. In service, we support. In service, we love.

Practice
Journal

To shift from our perception and mindset from sales to service, let's pull out the journal and reflect on the wisdom from teachers and servers:

- "Love your neighbor as yourself." —Jesus, the Gospel according to Mark
- "When you see yourself in others, it is impossible to hurt anyone else." —The Buddha
- "The world is transformed by those who love all people, just as you love yourself." —Lao Tzu, Tao Te Ching
- "The best way to find yourself is to lose yourself in the service of others." —Mahatma Gandhi

What are your thoughts about service? Fears? Hopes? Reflect on how you can serve others:

- At work
- At home
- In your community

Identify the Lack

A Course in Miracles teaches us *only what I am not giving can I be lacking.* Identify areas in your life you feel are lacking. How can you give in this area of lack? As you determine how you may serve others at work and in other areas of your life, look to ways you may integrate a service mindset. Areas leaders can serve and give include:

- Time
- Compassion
- Kindness
- Attention
- Love
- Resources
- Acceptance
- Support
- Acknowledgment
- Shared Value Statement

One of the best ways to give of your time and serve your organization or community is to design a shared value statement. To accomplish this exercise, have each person on the team go through the value exercise found in Lesson 4: Intention. When complete, ask members to share their values and facilitate a discussion so that all may fully understand the individual perceptions and mental models.

Once each team member has shared his or her individual values, complete the exercise again, this time as a team. Once the team identifies their collective top five values, review the organization's mission and vision statements to identify alignment with team values. If discrepancies or conflicting messages arise, explore possibilities as to why they disconnect. Is it time to revise the mission or vision? Once resolved, create a value statement for the team, integrating the team's top five values.

You can do this exercise in large organizations, beginning with small department teams. Once each department completes the exercise, a group representing all departments and different levels of the organization come together to complete the overall organization value statement. The benefit with this format is that each department has collectively identified shared values and participates in the final organizational values statement. Identifying the organizational values in this meaningful way brings the heart into the picture.

Vision and mission statements are great but sometimes do not touch us as deeply as our values. A combination of all three statements—vision, mission, and values—completes a holistic view of the organizational map.

As leaders collaborate and empower others, they experience great joy and satisfaction. In service, leaders find joy. As Goethe stated many years ago, "Who is the happiest of men? He who values the merits of others and in their pleasure takes joy, even as though it were his own."

Pause

You are now invited to pray, reflect, or meditate on . . .

Dear God,

through my service with others,

I serve you.

I give of myself with joy

my time,

attention,

and love.

Help me to see

the opportunities

you lay before me

to serve

for a higher purpose,

to your purpose,

to love.

Amen.

19
LESSON

FORGIVENESS

To forgive is the highest, most beautiful form of love. In return, you will receive untold peace and happiness.
—**Robert Muller**

Teachings, Thoughts, and Theories

Forgiveness is a challenging concept for many leaders. While we understand the idea and we know forgiveness when it happens, the vagueness surrounding forgiveness is elusive. The ambiguity enfolding forgiveness stems from our questions of how to bring about forgiveness and understanding, and from where it originated. To begin this lesson, let's take a dive into the word itself.

For implies intention to someone, for the benefit of or on behalf of someone or something. *Give* is to pass on, to gift, or convey something to someone. *Ness* is a suffix that implies a state of being. *For-give-ness*, therefore, is a state of benefiting someone by giving something to him or her. How did we even get here—the need or desire to forgive?

We look to practice forgiveness when we are angry, wronged, or hurt. Tormentors come in the form of resentment, guilt, or even shame. Oftentimes, we hold on to anger as a form of power. We feel in control and ultimately powerful when we hold onto our anger, justified in our feelings, and hoping that the person we believe hurt us may feel guilty or remorseful for what we perceive they have done to us. Avoiding forgiveness allows us to fuel our anger, feeling justified and entitled in our anger or pain as victims. This practice of avoidance may manifest by not communicating with the person who harmed us, furthering the growth of our anger. Avoiding forgiveness is avoiding responsibility. We are victims because we believe we have no power. Playing the victim role deepens the feelings of pain and anger justification. Each mental

> Avoiding forgiveness is avoiding responsibility.

replay of the event that caused us pain is another attempt to regain respect, acknowledgment, hope, and love.

Because forgiveness is a state of being, action is required to move into that place or that state. Like so many other lessons, avoiding forgiveness is not a static place. We are either moving into forgiveness or moving away from it. Anger leads to judgment. (*He was so mean, disrespectful, or vindictive when he did that to me. She is so arrogant that she didn't even realize she hurt me.*) Judgment leads to blame, and blame leads to resentment. Resentment is unresolved anger, and resentment hurts us, manifesting in stress-related illness, anxiety, or depression. Resentment hardens our hearts by paving a path of vengeance. We can lose ourselves in judgment, condemnation, and conflict, all the while wondering why we are not happy and content.

Illness resulting from stress leads to heart disease, digestive disorders, and suppressed immune systems. Psychologically, stress and resentment show up as depression and anxiety. Spiritually, we don't feel connected to God when filled with anger and resentment, and this separation is exactly what ego feeds on. As leaders, we must practice forgiveness first, for ourselves.

When we place our underlying anger and guilt onto another person, resentment shows up emotionally and psychologically as projection. What we are truly seeing in those moments are reflections of ourselves seeking acceptance and understanding.

Perceptions, as we know, can be false representations masking truth and love. Suppression is another manifestation of unresolved anger. Denial of anger and resentment is like pretending the feelings are nonexistent. Again, physical illness as well as an uneasy state of anxiety may result from denying our feelings of anger. Repression is a psychological condition of deeply set denial, so deep that we are not even conscious of the event. "All dis-ease comes from a state of un-forgiveness," *A Course in Miracles* tells us. We may experience these psychological and emotional effects of anger in an unbalanced nagging that eventually leads to hardening of our hearts.

Forgiveness is a choice. We take responsibility for our peace of mind and happiness when we choose to forgive. Many leaders think that if we forgive, it is for the benefit of others. But the primary beneficiary when one chooses to forgive is the *one who forgives*. The primary function is removing ego separation, thus bringing us back into our right mind with God. To make this choice, we experience a miracle.

The process of experiencing the miracle of forgiveness is perception shifting. The change in attitude comes to us through grace. Cultivating a practice of forgiveness first begins with self-forgiveness. Dr. Robin Casarjian describes six steps to practice self-forgiveness in her book, *Forgiveness*:[37]

1. Acknowledge the truth.

2. Take responsibility for what you have done.

3. Learn from the experience by acknowledging the deeper feelings that motivated the behaviors and thoughts for which you now feel guilty and hold yourself in judgment.

4. Open your heart to yourself and compassionately listen to the fears and calls for help and acknowledgment deep within.

5. Heal emotional wounds by heeding the calls in healthy, loving, and responsible ways.

6. Align with your Self and affirm your fundamental innocence.

By practicing self-forgiveness, always remember to be gentle with yourself, suspending judgment, allowing and receiving miracles in this holy space. The miracle and shift in perception and attitude gives us insight about others and ourselves.

Forgiving others benefits us, while compassionately demonstrating love for others. Family, coworkers, individuals, and groups are all potential targets of our reluctance to forgive because of hurt or anger. Harboring anger and resentment is toxic. Forgiveness of others releases the debilitating effects of this poison. When we examine anger, we find that anger is on the surface, and the deeper we go, the more we uncover the emotions and needs underlying our anger. We find ego and a cry for acknowledgment, respect, hope, and love. When we open to the healing miracle of forgiveness, we sometimes see other people as souls who did they best they could at the time, still on the path to love and wholeness with God. They, too, are crying out for love.

> Harboring anger and resentment is toxic. Forgiveness of others releases the debilitating effects of this poison.

It is important for us to know that other people's behavior has nothing to do with us; they are dealing with their own issues, manifested outwardly. As we explore forgiving others, we must know that forgiveness is not a license for others to abuse us. Forgiving others is not saying that their behavior is acceptable. The practice of forgiveness is for *our* freedom. Their behavior has nothing to do with us, and yet our act of forgiveness is one of the most powerful actions we can do. Reminding us of this power are the wise words of Mahatma Gandhi, "The weak can never forgive. Forgiveness is the attribute of the strong."

What ingredients do we need to practice forgiveness? We must suspend judgment and expectation. Why is it we get angry with others when they do not meet our expectations? We must see the ego living in the expectation, and instead turn toward truth and love.

Awareness, as we've discussed in many lessons, is foundational to this practice. Pouring awareness into our perceptions helps us recognize the pride and ego fueling our anger or resentment. Awareness helps us move beyond perceptions to recognize limiting beliefs we have about the person or their behavior. We are then able to release the burden of toxic thoughts, beliefs, and behavior patterns, thus breaking free from the chains of hurt and guilt.

Several years ago, I experienced the immense healing that comes from forgiveness. My mentor at the time, a person whom I trusted completely, betrayed my confidence, and I became extremely angry and resentful. I have always been a tenacious person, and, true to form, I held on to this anger for two years, letting it grow into full bitterness. Finally, heavy with the burden and toxic feelings, I decided to forgive him. The next time I saw him, I told him I forgave him for hurting me, and I apologized for my vengeful behavior. It really did not matter much to me if he accepted my apology because for the first time in my life, I realized that I forgave him for *me*. I could not believe how much lighter I felt—as though twenty pounds were gone. I was ready to fly and to soar to greater heights—and all I did was forgive him. While the relationship was never one of great trust again, forgiveness released me from the burden of anger and resentment, allowing us to build a congenial working relationship.

Forgiveness is like a resurrection, born again into love and a fresh start. Forgiveness is the road to joy, love, and peace. Like the beautiful Sanskrit term *namaste*, which means *I bow to you*, we love and honor the spirit of each other in truth.

Honesty and grace, too, are required ingredients for forgiveness. We must be honest both with ourselves and with others.

Remember that honesty is not an excuse to be hurtful. Far too many times I've heard leaders say hurtful words to other people under the guise of, "I'm just being honest." True honesty comes from love, and love does not hurt. Only in our egos do we experience separation from love and pain. With the 3 Cs of grace discussed in Lesson 10—care, compassion, and confidence—we may step into forgiveness. As we look to the rebirth forgiveness affords us, we are reminded by Desmond Tutu, "Without forgiveness, there's no future."

True honesty comes from love, and love does not hurt.

Practice

How do we develop the habit of forgiveness? Below are some exercises to help us live in the state of forgiveness.

Letting Go

Think of a situation where you feel stuck or find difficulty letting go of something (that nagging in your head and heart). Let's begin with naming the event and the people involved. Don't rush through this exercise; sit with your thoughts and emotions. Now list all the people in that scenario for whom you feel anger or resentment. Next to each name, identify the emotions you feel for that person. Again, do not rush through, but identify as many emotions as you feel with each individual. As you begin to peel away the emotional layers with each person, honor each emotion without shoving it back in. As you experience each feeling, visualize the emotion as a dandelion, white with wispy seeds. After you have fully experienced your emotions, look at the dandelion. Gently blow and watch the soft white seeds break away, leaving only the stem, releasing your emotions on each piece of the white seeds. Feel the freedom as the pieces blow away.

Blame Game

Identify those you blame or believe have contributed to a hurtful situation. List all those people you blame or feel anger or resentment toward. Do not rush through this exercise. I must admit how surprised I was the first time I did the exercise that I had to use more than one sheet of paper.

With each person on the list, visualize your highest self or soul knocking on the door of the person's highest self. When they answer their door, ask if you may come in. Be prepared if they say *no*, to come back again another time. Once in, sit down at the table with them and say everything you've wanted to say to them, listening with your entire being to their reactions and responses. Then, fully listen to them with your heart. When you both have completely expressed your feelings, thank the person and leave. As you leave, know that you are leaving behind all the unspoken thoughts and feelings that you previously held inside—they are now gone. You leave reborn and lighter.

Sometimes when we think about forgiving someone, we may resist because we don't want to subject ourselves to possible abuse or hurt from that person. Forgiveness does not call for us to be victims or used as doormats. We can forgive someone without ever seeing him or her again. The above visualizations do not require us to leave the safety of our own hearts and minds. Ours is a sacred space, safe and filled with love. Setting boundaries for others and ourselves is an important step in self-love, and we explore this further in Lesson 20: Relationships.

Honor and Love

Complete the above exercises with the focus on yourself and any regrets or guilt you may feel. Honor each emotion as in the previous exercises, and release them to the wind. Invite the Holy

Spirit into this sacred space, and feel the loving arms of God around you. Feel the safety and warmth of His love as He envelops you in the white light of forgiveness. Feel the miraculous rebirth of living in this state of forgiveness.

Pause

You are now invited to pray, reflect, or meditate on . . .

Dear God,

Thank you for lifting

the burdens, shackles, and chains

of my anger, bitterness, and resentment.

Into your arms

I lay my burdened heart.

Through the grace of

your Holy Spirit

You've un-hardened my heart

to receive

love,

joy,

peace,

and forgiveness.

Amen.

20
LESSON

RELATIONSHIPS

The most important single ingredient in the formula of success is knowing how to get along with people.

—**Theodore Roosevelt**

Strange is our situation here upon earth. Each of us comes for a short visit, not knowing why, yet sometimes seeming to divine a purpose. From the standpoint of daily life, however, there is one thing we do know: that man is here for the sake of other men.

—**Albert Einstein**

Teachings, Thoughts, and Theories

Wise leaders know that leading is all about relationships. We also know that many of the highs and lows we experience throughout our lifetime involve relationships. Why are relationships so important for leadership? Plain and simple, *we can't do it by ourselves*, and *it* is anything and everything.

Leaders sometimes confuse establishing relationships with connecting with people for the purposes of *buy-in*, conformity, and nonresistance. Leaders who are looking for buy-in and calling it a relationship have a misguided perception of a relationship. Relationships are an exchange, not a one-way interaction. The boss who addresses his or her team with information is not in a relationship but exhibits a one-way form of sharing information (like a classroom lecture).

Sometimes leaders think that buy-in ensures engagement, which is true—for a while. As discussed in Lesson 18: Service, leaders are much more effective with a servant mindset over a sales mindset. The sales mindset looks for buy-in, whereas the service mindset looks for how to best support the followers, which in turn creates follower engagement. To be an effective leader, we must create our authentic relationships and connect with our team and our followers.

Relationships require two main actions: connecting and nurturing. Connecting with others requires authenticity. Lack of authenticity is one of the primary wedges driven between people; we can smell *fake* a mile away. When our leaders are not authentic, we do not trust them, and when we do not trust, we do not engage. Authenticity shows our humanness and our vulnerability. Living in authenticity is living in truth, revealing our frailty and our strength. We are not perfect, so let's stop trying to convince others and ourselves that we are.

In our interactions with each other, we connect and nurture our relationships by actively listening to one another. Active listening, or power listening, is extremely effective because we use all our senses, including intuition. This active listening, as discussed in Lesson 5: Power Listening, fills our mind both with what the other person is saying and

Authenticity shows our humanness and our vulnerability.

what they are not saying. We become fully present and mindful in that interchange, which connects us. We serve each other, not looking for what we can get from the other but only asking what we can offer. Demonstrating our gratitude and appreciation outwardly shows how we honor and acknowledge each other. Blessed attention to these relationships is our demonstration of love-based leadership.

One of my clients, a chief operating officer (COO) at a utility company, came to me because his direct reports and team members said that he was unapproachable, and the CEO told him that he needed to be an active listener. The COO did not know what that meant, and he was eager to learn that skill. Once we started exploring the challenge he had in his relationships, I realized that active listening was simply a part of a larger issue. The COO had not taken any time to build relationships throughout the organization, especially with his direct reports. He thought that going out into the field and having conversations was not what he was "being paid to do." However, that was EXACTLY what he was being paid to do. When you are in a leadership role, you are expected to LEAD. You cannot lead if you do not have any followers. The most sustainable way to have followers helping you move in the direction of the mission and vision is to have trusting, substantive relationships with those whom you lead. Period. When he realized the importance of building relationships and used the active listening skills he learned, his relationships started turning around within weeks. He scheduled time on his calendar to go into the field, have conversations, and get to know his people. He even shared with me a few comments he received from his colleagues about what a great listener he was!

Choosing honesty and integrity with ourselves and with others is another way to connect with our team and followers. Integrity demonstrated is a tremendous trust builder. Trust in relationships is a key ingredient. People will trust us when we are honest and do what we say we are going to do. We earn respect through integrity, and in a relationship, respect is like using Miracle-Gro on a flower. This nutrient will grow the relationship in meaning and deeper respect.

Another way to nurture relationships is with our time. Spending time getting to know our team members increases our connection with them, all the while nurturing our relationships. By handling our relationships with tender loving care, we will see strong connections grow, increasing our leadership capacity with influence. Treating others with care, compassion, love, and kindness are all nutrients to grow and nurture strong relationships.

> By handling our relationships with tender loving care, we will see strong connections grow, increasing our leadership capacity with influence.

Even though this is an older example, it remains one of my favorites! Below is a full-page advertisement found in *USA Today* on Boss's Day in 1994. This ad was for the late Herb Kelleher, cofounder and then CEO of Southwest Airlines (LUV airline), and demonstrates the power of connection in relationships:

Thanks Herb,

For remembering every one of our names. For supporting the Ronald McDonald House. For helping load baggage on Thanksgiving.

For giving everyone a kiss (and we mean everyone).

For listening.

For singing only once a year.

For letting us wear shorts and sneakers to work.

For golfing at the LUV Classic with only one club.

For outtalking Sam Donaldson.

For riding your Harley Davidson into Southwest Headquarters. For being a friend, not just a boss.

Happy Boss' Day from Each One of Your 16,000 Employees.

Let's take this even deeper. Love-based leaders connect with their team and with their followers through love. When we approach relationships with love, and not in fear, they are *holy* relationships. *A Course in Miracles* describes the difference between *special relationships* and *holy relationships*. *Special*, or unholy, relationships recognize differences, with one person possessing something that the other person does not have but they desire to obtain. These special relationships are simply *transactional* relationships. At its most basic level, one person gives something to another person in order to receive a benefit for themselves—regardless of the impact upon the other person. Special relationships thrive upon division and separateness, hence making them special or transactional.

Anything that divides us is from the ego, as the ego exists to separate, specifically to separate us from God. Special relationships have a distorted perception of love, requiring that we seek love outside of ourselves and through other people. In special relationships, we do not feel whole or complete without the other. The danger to us is that when we feel fearful of losing this "love," we attempt to hide and mask our real selves in our attempt to hold on to the love. Judgment, expectation, and conditions surround special relationships.

Holy relationships start from a different foundational concept, with each one seeing the other as whole, lacking nothing. Miracles occur when special relationships transform to holy relationships through the Holy Spirit, shifting perceptions from judgment and separation to acceptance and wholeness. When we have holy relationships, we are committed to each other and to our highest self. This is the ultimate in leadership—leading with purpose.

Holy relationships, because they come from love, are authentic and solid. As leaders, it is important to treat holy relationships with sacred, loving care. These relationships are consciously connected and are powerful. When fear starts to creep in, recognize it as ego and return to love. Because we are spiritual beings having a human experience, we make mistakes. In holy relationships, we do not condemn each other, but learn and move on. Forgiveness, empathy, care, and compassion are key ingredients in establishing holy relationships. These are the ingredients we experience with God, and these ingredients will fill our relationships with joy, peace, and tremendous fulfillment.

Sometimes other people in our lives are not ready, willing, or able to enter into holy relationships, and oftentimes those relationships become harmful. Created in and for love, we recognize that sometimes love for ourselves requires us to redesign certain relationships. When others abuse us, reminders of acceptable and unacceptable behavior are in order. If the behavior is not acceptable to us, we do not need to stick around for the second act. We may have love for someone and choose to avoid being physically around him or her. When we have a holy relationship with our Self, the love, honor, and care that we have for ourselves is stronger than the need for a special relationship with someone who harms us.

I once worked with a company president who demanded that his executive staff socialize outside of work with him and with each other. This was a forced special relationship, inauthentic and harmful. I was once reprimanded for not attending a company party where the atmosphere at the party made me uncomfortable. I realized that the love I had for myself was stronger than my love of that job, and left shortly thereafter.

Relationships that do not live in this holy space sometimes occur within our families and among friends. As we move closer to love's full embrace, the ego gets extremely nervous and goes into overdrive. Ego in relationships manifests through jealousy, envy, control, abuse, judgment, guilt, and any emotion or behavior resulting from fear. Healing can occur through the Holy Spirit, replacing fear with love. Even with forgiveness, we sometimes need to remove ourselves from situations that cause us harm and then redesign the relationship to be one of love with distance.

Leaders sometimes struggle with concepts of spirituality concerning work relationships. Work relationships are really *work contracts*. The relationships we have with others, whether at work or outside of work, may still be either holy or special relationships. The work contracts are like social contracts that define work performance and behavior expectations. Do not confuse the work contract expectations with expectations of the ego in special relationships. When an employee does not perform the work for which he or she was "contracted," the leader has a responsibility to address this issue.

One of the top reasons for conflict in the workplace is a lack of clearly defined roles and expectations. We can still maintain a holy relationship at work by addressing the work performance or behavior as just that, *performance* or *behavior*, and not the wholeness or perceived lack of wholeness of the person. With a holy relationship, love, care, and compassion are present in the discussion of missed expectation in work performance or behavior. In a holy relationship, both the leader and the team member take self-responsibility in work contract expectations.

To live our spiritual lives does not mean that we are not responsible. Actually, it means precisely the opposite—we are called to live our highest self, and with that mission follows responsibility, initiative, and accountability. Living a spiritual life is not a lazy life—it is a life of fullness, wholeness, and love.

When our relationships are strong and holy, our relationship with God grows to profound heights.

Practice
Your Circle

We begin this practice by looking at the following relationships:

- God/Universe/Source
- Self
- Romantic partner
- Family
- Friends
- Coworkers
- Community

Examine these relationships, and list those who are in your circle. Identify those within your sphere of influence. Which relationships are special? Which are holy? What do you want from these relationships? What do you want to give to these relationships? How do you nurture your relationships? How do you want to nurture them? Do you have clearly defined work contracts? If not, how can you define the work contract expectations for performance and behavior?

With any special relationships you identified, what is preventing those relationships from being holy ones? Is blame, judgment, fear, or guilt blocking or stifling the relationship? Is forgiveness necessary? You may want to revisit the forgiveness visualizations in Lesson 19: Forgiveness to help heal the relationship.

Remember that with God, all things are possible. Our relationships are beacons of God's love throughout the world.

Pause

You are now invited to pray, reflect, or meditate on . . .
Dear God,

Thank you for the holy relationship.

I know that from you,

with you,

and in you

is pure love.

May I grow in the spirit

of loving relationships

with those I lead,

with myself,

and always

with you.

Amen.

21
LESSON
LOVE

*If you want what visible reality can give,
you are an employee. If you want the unseen
world, you are not living with your truth.
Both wishes are foolish, but you'll be forgiven
for forgetting that what you really want is
love's confusing joy.*

—Rumi

Teachings, Thoughts, and Theories

Love, indeed, is all we want. However, we sure have complicated that notion. I often wonder why, in our inherent quest for love, that we turn from it every chance we get. The answer is too simple: it's scary—*fear*. Fear, the antithesis of love, stems from the ego. Remember that the ego's primary function is to separate, and fear is the vehicle ego uses to accomplish this goal. Lucky for us, love is stronger than fear.

Love is the critical element in leading our countries, organizations, communities, and our lives in this new era. "The great paradox of the 21st century is that, in this age of powerful technology, the biggest problems we face internationally are problems of the human soul," said author Ralph Peters. By choosing to live our lives in love and awareness, our soul wakes up to the glorious gifts of life.

When we let love in, we remove the darkness from our souls.

In our choice to live in love, we must first wake up to and recognize fear and ego. The ego is slick, subtle, and oh, so smart.

When we feel jealousy of a friend's success or feel comfort because of someone's misfortune, we may think, *At least I am better off than that*, and we must know that these are thoughts from the underbelly of the ego. This is the shadow of ego and fear woven so tightly in the fabric of our lives that we do not recognize it as such.

Our curiosity is sometimes piqued by the spectacle of another's misfortune. Television shows and websites exist with the singular objective of showing unattractive photos of celebrities or "worst-dressed" images. These negative thoughts and images are food for the ego and are attempts to keep us in the darkness of our souls. Ego does this so easily with our emotions, too, encouraging us to shove feelings deep inside our bodies, masking the light of our souls. "Darkness is the absence of light, and fear is the absence of love," wrote Marianne Williamson in *A Return to Love*. When we let love in, we remove the darkness from our souls.

Fear also manifests as negativity. With negativity, we often feel that we have lost power, and the only way to retain power is to exercise complaints. Criticism is also cleverly disguised fear. We criticize to gain attention and to build our esteem, albeit falsely, but that is the cleverness of FEAR—**F**alse **E**vidence **A**ppearing **R**eal. We see fear manifested through overly aggressive as well as overly agreeable behavior, both stemming from the need for love and attention. Cruelty is an overt form of fear, striking out and often preying upon seemingly defenseless targets. Manipulation is ego's smooth work of fear. If we peel back the layers of these manifestations of fear, we find the same underlying need for love.

Why do we run from love and let fear rule? We run from love because love requires authenticity and vulnerability, and we are fearful that others *won't love us if they knew who we really are.* The irony in that statement is that who we really are is *perfect love.* Perfect love.

Love is the miraculous shift from separation to oneness. This makes our ego nervous. We cannot experience more than one emotion at a time, so either we are in a state of fear or in a state of love. The choice is ours; and that choice we know as *free will.* We don't get to write the script of fear or love, but we get to choose how we live in either state. We were born with and we learned fear throughout our life. The beautiful lesson of our lives is that we get to wake up to this awareness and know that we have the extreme power to choose. Love is transformational. Love is a miracle.

David Hawkins shared results of his study in *Power vs. Force*, where he measured levels of human consciousness and the energy fields to which they were connected.[38] He localized a range of values and their corresponding sets of emotions. Hawkins placed the energy field values on a scale of 1–1,000 with 1,000 at the highest level and 1 at the lowest. His incredible results are below:

Value	Energy Level	Emotion
Enlightenment	700–1,000	Ineffable
Peace	600	Bliss
Joy	540	Serenity
Love	500	Reverence
Reason	400	Understanding
Acceptance	350	Forgiveness
Willingness	310	Optimism
Neutrality	250	Trust
Courage	200	Affirmation
Pride	175	Scorn
Anger	150	Hate
Desire	125	Craving
Fear	100	Anxiety
Grief	75	Regret
Apathy	50	Despair
Guilt	30	Blame

Hawkins's chart shows that love and the resulting feelings of joy, peace, and enlightenment vibrate at the highest frequencies. Fear and the feelings of grief, apathy, and guilt vibrate at the lowest end. Is it any wonder why those lower-frequency emotions drain us while love energizes us? Is this not something you would want to infuse into your organization, family, community, or world?

When we infuse love into our workplaces and our lives, we experience great accomplishments. Rev. Dr. Martin Luther King Jr. often spoke of how Mahatma Gandhi lifted love into a political and social force. Love and the resultant passion move mountains and heals masses. Love is transformational, and is precisely what we need to wake up our souls, understand our purpose, and bring meaning back into the workplace, our communities, and our lives. The time has come for us to decompartmentalize our lives and lead with a holistic perspective. When we lead with purpose, we discover joy, passion, meaning, and yes, *love*.

As I wrote in *Love-Based Leadership*, the leadership model of love is based on three pillars: love of Self, love of Source, and love of Others. This holistic approach recognizes that we are whole beings, and in order to lead with authenticity, we must bring our entire self to work. Recognizing the destructive effects of fear-based leadership, the love-based leadership (LBL) model offers an approach steeped in right-mindedness. Only love is real.

Love of Self is the first pillar of LBL. Self-love, as described in Lesson 14: Health, is not arrogance, but one of tender loving care of our mind, body, and soul. Taking care of our body temple and nourishing our mind and soul will keep us at our optimum, regardless of our physical age. This requires a decompartmentalized approach to living and leading, so we must begin first with ourselves. Self-love uses all the lessons we've learned in this course, reaching toward our highest self. Developing and harnessing intuition, living in truth and integrity, shifting perception, remaining in a state of openness, and being aware comprise some of the lessons learned in this course preparing us to lead with love.

Love of Source is oneness with God, our endless source of love, compassion, and wisdom. Nurturing our relationship with Him requires only that we stop, be still, and know. We can also maintain an awareness of His presence through the Holy Spirit throughout our day. My favorite times with God are the still moments, showered in love, so much so that I get chills throughout my body. The radiance of love fills me with an endless flow of joy and contentment. Our reconnection with God, our soul's primary purpose, finds fulfillment in love.

Love of Others is a natural extension when we align with self-awareness and God. Love, care, trust, and compassion are all elements necessary for knowledge creation, motivation, and purpose as we discussed in several lessons. This is not a *kumbaya* way to lead. On the contrary, leading with love creates strong, healthy, and meaningful work environments where innovation and creativity thrive.

When employees know they are cared about and loved, they will trust their leadership, and an environment of love replaces one of fear. How do we create an LBL environment? We celebrate each other, with joy and support. We welcome different perspectives to give well-thought-out solutions and innovations. We practice gratitude and forgiveness. We teach each other and learn from one another. We discover meaning and purpose, encouraging others to discover on their own. We move from blame to accountability, routine to awareness, and scarcity to abundance. We bring together all of the lessons we have learned to lead with love.

Practice
Journal Reflection

To cultivate a love-based leadership approach, we begin with reflection. Stop and listen to your thoughts. What are your barriers to love? What resistance shows up? Sit with any fears masquerading as doubt, criticism, or negativity. Write down these thoughts and feelings, while digging deeper to uncover the underlying fears. Are you afraid to be vulnerable? Imagine what is the worst thing that could happen in your vulnerability, and then ask yourself the five questions we learned in Lesson 6: Openness.

Dr. Dyer's Overcoming Ego

Dr. Wayne Dyer describes seven steps for overcoming ego's hold in his book *The Power of Intention:*[39]

1. Stop being offended.

2. Let go of your need to win.

3. Let go of your need to be right.

4. Let go of your need to be superior.

5. Let go of your need to have more.

6. Let go of identifying yourself based on your achievements.

7. Let go of your reputation. [Do not let others define you.]

Deeper Reflection

Explore and reflect on the following questions and journal your responses. Do not rush through these exercises.

▶ What affect does fear have in your life? How has it paralyzed you?

▶ What impact has love had in your life? When are the times you've been resistant to love?

▶ How has love energized you?

▶ How do you demonstrate self-love? List three specific ways you practice self-love or plan to practice self-love.

▶ How do you nurture your love of Source? Do you have a special place for prayer or meditation? Is this part of your daily routine? List three specific ways you connect with your Source or plan to cultivate this connection.

▶ How do you practice love of others? List three specific ways you demonstrate love to and with other people.

The Plan

As you determine your plan for the above questions, remember to use SMART goals from Lesson 15: Growth (**S**pecific, **M**easurable, **A**ligned with your values, **R**ealistic, and **T**ime-bound), and find an accountability partner or coach to help you stay on target.

As you practice leading with love, be prepared for ego to try to mess things up. With awareness, you will recognize ego's attempt to inject fear in one of its many forms. In those moments of awareness, stop, close your eyes, and take three deep breaths. Visualize, with each breath, love entering your lungs, and with each exhale, visualize fear pushed out. This practice will center you and invite the Holy Spirit back into your sacred heart.

Lead only with love.

Pause

You are now invited to pray, reflect, or meditate on . . .

Dear God,

As we enter a new era,

infuse our workplaces,

our homes,

our communities,

our countries,

and our lives

with your healing

and illuminating love.

I choose to be

a beacon of love,

hope,

joy,

and peace.

Amen.

A CALL TO LEADERS: A CALL TO HEARTS

I am coming to feel that the people of ill will have used time much more effectively than the people of goodwill. We will have to repent in this generation not merely for the vitriolic words and actions of the bad people, but for the appalling silence of the good people. We must come to see that human progress never rolls in on wheels of inevitability. It comes through the tireless efforts and persistent work of men [and women] willing to be coworkers with God, and without this hard work time itself becomes an ally of the forces of social stagnation. We must use time creatively, and forever realize that the time is always ripe to do right.

—Rev. Dr. Martin Luther King Jr.

There is a movement emerging in our culture. We may call this era, this time and place, an *evolution in leadership*. In fact, this shift in consciousness is so important to leaders across the globe, inciting passionate changes in the way we lead, that we may even call it a *revolution*—a leadership revolution with a call to hearts.

Historically, a revolution is a revolt, an uprising against the standard or status quo. As unemployed workers reenter the workplace, wounded and weary, they are skeptical of leaders and organizations. The uprising against the status quo is ubiquitous as we see organizations and leaders worldwide joining the leadership revolution. Leaders are recognizing the power of this shift, and wise leaders are getting on board, finding great results in their organizations within this movement. They are experiencing increased morale, productivity, and business results. Leaders are shifting from competition to collaboration, coercion to influence, secrecy to transparency, information gathering to information distribution, scarcity to abundance, and fear to love—and this is only the beginning.[40]

We are creating new models of leadership and teaching with love; yet the concepts are as ancient as was written in the *Book of History*, the *Shu Ching*, "Those who seek mentoring, will rule the great expanse under heaven. Those who boast that they are greater than others, will fall short. Those who are willing to learn from others, become greater. Those who are ego-involved, will be humbled and made small." To lead, we must follow; and to love, we must turn from ego.

Lao Tzu taught three leadership qualities:[41]

1. Compassion for all creatures

2. Material simplicity or frugality

3. A sense of equality or modesty

We have learned these qualities in our lessons on *compassion, grace, order, health,* and *relationships.* Each one of the leadership qualities that Lao Tzu described come from love, and only from love. Lao Tzu recognized that leaders model spiritual behavior and live in integrity with their values, aligning behavior, thoughts, and attitudes, requiring rising above the ego and into God's grace. Leaders who embody these qualities know the importance of bringing people together, providing leadership development and encouragement.

Leaders also provide an environment conducive to knowledge creation and innovation, free from the fear of failure. Leaders with these qualities help their teams discover meaningful work environments, discovering their higher purpose and greater good.

As we come to the end of this course, let us remember that the Course in Leadership never ends. We must continue to learn and grow in deeper understanding of others, our Source, and ourselves. I like to conclude my courses and my coaching sessions with an assessment, just as we did when we began. To assist you with setting up your action plans, visit *www.ACourseInLeadership.com* where you will find tools and additional activities. With awareness and reflection, please answer the following questions:

▶ What have you learned from this course?

▶ How will you apply these concepts in your life?

▶ What immediate three steps can you take to create the life you choose?

▶ What will it take to create your ideal organization?

► What immediate three steps can you take to create your ideal organization?

► What immediate three steps can you take to create a shift from fear to love in your community?

Take the responses to the above questions and create an action plan using the following ten steps:

1. Identify your goals, remembering to use the SMART goal framework from Lesson 15: Growth. For each of your SMART goals, apply the following steps:

2. List the necessary steps you need to achieve your goal.

3. List past success or strengths to remind you that you can achieve the goal.

4. List people or resources you have available for support.

5. List strengths, support, and resources upon which you could draw if you stumble.

6. List any weaknesses or blocks that could potentially cause you to stumble.

7. List the value, reasons, and benefits that propel your desire to achieve the goal.

8. Describe in great detail what the end state of achieving each goal looks and feels like.

9. Celebrate!

10. Find a coach or an accountability partner to work with you on keeping your commitment.

We are rising in consciousness, waking from our slumber, and coming into our best selves. As we evolve into love-based leadership, we ready our collective selves to resurrect the best within us. As we break **Leadership is love.**

free from our own fear, we invite others to do the same. *We must not forget this.*

Leadership is responsibility. Leadership is accountability. Leadership is love.

Pause

You are now invited to pray, reflect, or meditate on . . .

Dear God,

Thank you for this holy instant.

Thank you for this holy relationship.

Thank you for your Holy Spirit.

Thank you for love.

Bless all who lead

with your grace and peace.

Thank you for the collection of hearts

as we lead lives,

communities,

organizations,

and nations in love.

Amen.

"And may the holy instant speed you on the way, as it will surely do if you but let it come to you." ~ *A Course in Miracles*

See you on the path. Namaste.

Additional Resources

To download your bonus material and complimentary companion Action Guide to *A Course in Leadership: 21 Spiritual Lessons on Power, Love, and Influence*, please visit *www.ACourseInLeadership.com*

For more information about Love-Based Leadership, please visit: *www.LoveBasedLeadership.com* or *www.DrMaria Church.com*.

Dr. Maria TV leadership videos at *http://www.youtube.com/c/Drmariachurchtv*.

To work with Dr. Maria Church and her extraordinary team:
www.CorporateLeadershipSolutions.com
www.GovernmentLeadershipSolutions.com
www.LeadershipDevelopmentUniversity.com

I would love to hear about your Love-Based Leadership experiences. Please contact me at *Maria@DrMariaChurch.com*.

Acknowledgments

With sincere gratitude, I wish to thank my team for their support as I "checked out" to write, especially Marie Gacke and Colleen Dorame. Thank you Gail Woodard and the wonderful team at Dudley Court Press for pushing me to get the absolute best.

With my heart full of peace and love, I am so grateful for my mother and father, Donna and Sal Jaime. Thank you for the freedom to explore life in many directions. Melissa, my beautiful daughter, I am profoundly grateful for your constant support and unconditional love. My amazing husband Brian, from the depths of my heart and soul, I thank you for your incredible support and patience as I completed this labor of love. I will love you 'til the stars fall from the sky. My Source, my God, I am forever grateful for your divine inspiration in leadership, love, and life.

Endnotes

[1] Maria Church, *Love-Based Leadership* and *10th Anniversary Edition of Love-Based Leadership.*

[2] Rev. Dr. Martin Luther King Jr., "My Pilgrimage to Nonviolence."

[3] Neville Goddard reminds us in *The Power of Awareness.*

[4] Iyanla Vanzant talk in Detroit.

[5] Viktor Frankl stated in *Man's Search for Meaning.*

[6] Frances Vaughan wrote in *Awakening Intuition.*

[7] Carlos Castaneda quoted by Wayne Dyer in *The Power of Intention.*

[8] Wayne Dyer in *The Power of Intention.*

[9] Maslow's Hierarchy of Needs in *The Farther Reaches of Human Nature.*

[10] Nonaka and Nishiguchi, *Knowledge Emergence.*

[11] Maslow, *The Farther Reaches of Human Nature.*

[12] Catherine D. Fyock, "Retention Tactics That Work." SHRM White Paper, 2002.

[13] Dale Carnegie, *How to Win Friends and Influence People.*

[14] Kent M. Keith, *Anyway.*

[15] Peter Senge, *The Fifth Discipline.*

[16] Marianne Williamson, *A Return to Love.*

[17] Earl Nightingale, *The Strangest Secret.*

[18] Matthew McKay, Martha Davis, and Patrick Fanning, *Thoughts & Feelings.*

[19] Viktor Frankl, *Man's Search for Meaning.*

[20] Several studies conducted by Dr. Robert Emmons and Dr. Michael McCullough.

[21] B. F. Skinner's theory of Behavior Modification.

[22] Viktor Frankl, *Man's Search for Meaning.*

[23] Wayne Dyer, *The Power of Intention.*

[24] This quote is often cited as being said by Voltaire. However, there is some debate that H. L. Mencken may be the originator of this statement.

[25] Daniel Pink, *A Whole New Mind.*

[26] Edward de Bono, *How to Have Creative Ideas.*

[27] Gail Blanke, *Throw Out 50 Things.*

[28] Marie Kondo, *The Life-Changing Magic of Tidying Up.*

[29] Daniel Amen, MD, *Success* magazine.

[30] Seth Godin, *Tribes.*

[31] Peter Senge, *The Fifth Discipline.*

[32] Nonaka and Nishiguchi, *Knowledge Emergence.*

[33] Peter Senge, *The Fifth Discipline.*

[34] Kahlil Gibran, *The Prophet.*

[35] Raven and French 5 Power Bases theory.

[36] Earl Shorris, *Scenes from Corporate Life.*

[37] Robin Casarjian, *Forgiveness.*

[38] David Hawkins shared results of his study in *Power vs. Force.*

[39] Wayne Dyer, *The Power of Intention.*

[40] William Craig, *Forbes* article, "As Company Culture Improves, So Does Your Business," March 2018.

[41] John Heider, *The Tao of Leadership.*

254 A Course in Leadership

Bibliography

A Course in Miracles. Mill Valley, CA: Foundation for Inner Peace, 1996.

Agor, Weston H. *Intuitive Management: Integrating Left and Right Brain Management Skills*. Englewood Cliff, NJ: Prentice-Hall, 1984.

Amen, Daniel. "Develop a Leader's Mind." *Success*. July 9, 2012. https://www.success.com/develop-a-leaders-mind/.

Blanke, Gail. *Throw Out Fifty Things: Clear the Clutter, Find Your Life*. New York, NY: Grand Central Life & Style, 2009.

Block, Peter. *Stewardship*. San Francisco, CA: Berrett-Koehler Publishers, Inc, 1996.

Carnegie, Dale. *How to Win Friends & Influence People*. New York, NY: Simon & Schuster, 1981.

Casarjian, Robin. *Forgiveness: A Bold Choice for a Peaceful Heart*. New York, NY: Bantam, 1992.

Church, Maria. *10th Anniversary Edition Love-Based Leadership: The Model for Strength, Grace, and Authenticity*. Sonoita, AZ: Dudley Court Press, 2020.

Church, Maria. *Intuition, Leadership, and Decision Making: A Phenomenon*. ProQuest, 2005.

Church, Maria. *Love-Based Leadership: Transform Your Life with Meaning and Abundance*. Bloomington, IN: Balboa Press, 2010.

Craig, William. "As Company Culture Improves, So Does Your Business." *Forbes*. March 6, 2018.

De Bono, Edward. *How to Have Creative Ideas: 62 Games to Develop the Mind*. London: Vermilion, 2008.

Dyer, Wayne W. *The Power of Intention: Learning to Co-create Your World Your Way*. Carlsbad, CA: Hay House, Inc, 2004.

Emmons, R. A. & McCullough, M. E. "Counting Blessings versus Burdens: An Experimental Investigation of Gratitude and Subjective Well-Being in Daily Life." *Journal of Personality and Social Psychology* 84, no. 2 (2003): 377–389.

Frankl, Viktor E. *Man's Search for Meaning*. New York, NY: Simon & Schuster, 1984.

Fyock, Catherine D. "Retention Tactics that Work." SHRM White Paper, 2002.

Gibran, Kahlil. *The Prophet*. New York, NY: Alfred A. Knopf, Inc, 1984.

Gladwell, Malcolm. *Blink: The Power of Thinking Without Thinking*. New York, NY: Little, Brown and Company, 2005.

Goddard, Neville. *The Power of Awareness*. Camarillo, CA: DeVorss & Company, 1992.

Godin, Seth. *Tribes: We Need You to Lead Us*. New York, NY: Penguin Group, 2008.

Hawkins, David R. *Power vs. Force: The Hidden Determinants of Human Behavior*. Carlsbad, CA: Hay House, Inc, 2002.

Heider, John. *The Tao of Leadership*. Atlanta, GA: Humanics New Age, 1997.

Kabat-Zinn, Jon. *Mindfulness for Beginners*. Boulder, CO: Sounds True, Inc., 2012.

Kent, Keith. *Anyway: Finding Personal Meaning in a Crazy World*. New York, NY: G.P. Putnam's Sons, 2001.

King, Rev. Dr. Martin Luther Jr. "My Pilgrimage to Nonviolence." Stanford University. September 1, 1958. https://kinginstitute. stanford.edu/king-papers/documents/my-pilgrimage-nonviolence.

Kondo, Marie. *The Life-changing Magic of Tidying Up: The Japanese Art of Decluttering and Organizing*. New York: Ten Speed Press, 2014.

Maslow, Abraham, H. *The Farther Reaches of Human Nature*. New York, NY: Penguin, 1976.

McKay, Matthew, Martha Davis, and Patrick Fanning. *Thoughts and Feelings: Taking Control of Your Moods and Your Life*. Oakland, CA: New Harbinger Publications, 2011.

McKenna, Jed. *Spiritual Enlightenment: The Damnedest Thing.* Fairfield, IA: Wisefool Press, 2010.

Mintzberg, Henry. "Planning on the Left Side and Managing on the Right." *Harvard Business Review* 54, no. 4 (July/August 1976): 49–58.

Nightingale, Earl. *The Strangest Secret.* Audio Recording. Wheeling, IL: Nightingale-Conant, 1986.

Nonaka, Ikujiro and Toshihiro Nishiguchi. *Knowledge Emergence: Social, Technical, and Evolutionary Dimensions of Knowledge Creation.* New York, NY: Oxford Press, 2001.

Pink, Daniel H. *A Whole New Mind: Why Right-Brainers Will Rule the Future.* New York, NY: Berkley Publishing Group, 2006.

Plato. *Meno.* As written in *Human Knowledge: Classic and Contemporary Approaches* by Paul K. Moser and Arnold vander Nat. New York, NY: Oxford University Press, 2003.

Sayings of White Eagle. *The Quiet Mind.* Great Britain: Oxford University Press, 1988.

Senge, Peter. *The Fifth Discipline: The Art and Practice of the Learning Organization.* New York, NY: Currency Doubleday, 1994.

Shorris, Earl. *Scenes from a Corporate Life.* New York, NY: Penguin, 1984.

Vanzant, Iyanla. Iyanla Live! Back to Basics. Simon & Schuster Audio, 2001.

Vaughan, Frances E. *Awakening Intuition.* New York, NY: Anchor Books, 1973.

Williamson, Marianne. *A Return to Love: Reflections on the Principles of A Course in Miracles.* New York, NY: HarperPerennial, 1996.

Index

All numbers are alphabetized as if spelled out; for example, 80/20 rule entry will appear between ego and elegance in the index.

Dr. Maria Church

Dr. Maria Church is CEO of Dr. Maria Church International, including both government and corporate divisions, and Leadership Development University. Starting the movement to revolutionize  the workplace with a shift from fear to love, she is the author of best-seller *The 10th Anniversary Edition of Love-Based Leadership: The Model for Leading with Strength, Grace, and Authenticity, Love-Based Leadership: Transform Your Life with Meaning and Abundance*, and co-author of the best-selling book, *Answering the Call*.

Dr. Church specializes in organizational culture, change agility, and leadership development with over twenty-five years working with Fortune 500, local governments, nonprofits, and academia. Her organizational culture work has realized her clients over 300% ROI, intentionally shaping their cultures to support strategic objectives and be a differentiator in the marketplace. Maria holds a Doctor of Management degree in Organizational Leadership and currently teaches for several universities. She is also part of the elite 17% worldwide who have earned a CSP (Certified Speaking Professional) designation from the National Speakers Association and speaks to world-wide audiences about leading with love.

Maria can almost always be found with her nose in a book, or an ear to classic rock playing air drums (she's hoping to learn drums from Keith Moon and Benny Benjamin in rock 'n' roll heaven). Splitting her time between Scottsdale and the canyons of southern Arizona, Maria continues to work with high-performing local governments, nonprofits, and private organizations. She is working on her next book about exemplary corporate and local government cultures.

Connect with Dr. Maria Church at:

www.DrMariaChurch.com

https://www.linkedin.com/in/drmariachurch/

https://www.facebook.com/dr.maria.church/

https://twitter.com/DrMariaChurch

http://www.youtube.com/c/Drmariachurchtv

https://www.instagram.com/drmariachurch/

More By Maria Church

Love-Based Leadership
The Model for Leading with Strength, Grace, and Authenticity

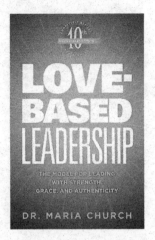

In a world where leadership doesn't always know where we are headed, knowing how to get there can be even more challenging. In Loved Based Leadership, Dr. Maria Church builds and expands on her successful Loved Based Leadership model developed a decade ago. In this 10th Anniversary Edition, she explores the need for leadership based not on fear or intimidation, but on respect for self, respect for others, honor, and integrity. The need for care over competition is emphasized in a leadership style that rewards success while establishing an environment that cherishes individuality, support, and a safe and loving environment.

Based on the three pillars of Love of Self, Love of Source, and Love of Others, Dr. Church's book outlines not only the how but also the why of a leadership model built on what helps us succeed in life and business. Loved Based Leadership nurtures our souls and fulfills needs outside of the workplace, giving us a sense of fulfillment and purpose. This is the leadership model that can forever change how authentic leadership is perceived.

Love Based Leadership shares powerful insights on increasing power by sharing it and how to rebuild your organization's leadership structure to strengthen it from within. The importance of trust, inspiration, and compassion and how they lead to innovation and success are outlined in Church's revelatory guide to leadership for a new age of leaders. She has created a new way forward for the best possible leader you can be in a world that longs for compassion as well as success.